Friends of the Earth Scotland's
Green Home Handbook

by Mark Sydenham

Friends of the Earth Scotland is committed to the conservation, restoration and sustainable use of the environment for the benefit of the community.

Friends of the Earth Scotland's
Green Home Handbook

Author	Mark Sydenham
Directory	Lorraine Dollin
Design	Oliver Brookes
Layout	Speedy B Designs
Contributions	George Baxter, Dr Richard Dixon, Angus Watt
Production	Catherine Bernard

ISBN 0 9506157 8 1

Publisher Friends of the Earth Scotland

72 Newhaven Road Edinburgh EH6 6QG

tel 0131 554 9977 fax 0131 554 8656

Published with support from The Scottish Office, Forward Scotland

Printing by Hay Nisbet Press

Paper Smith Anderson are pleased to sponsor the Green Home Handbook which is printed on Savatree recycled offset made by Smith Anderson from 100% post consumer waste. Cover 250 micron. Inside pages 100 gsm

This book is dedicated to the memory of Mark Smith (1973-1996)

Contents

Before Reading On

With this handbook you can do your best to reduce the environmental impact of your home. Section two highlights many of the global environmental issues that we can do something about by making changes at home, and specific issues are covered throughout the book, cross referenced wherever appropriate. It may seem that some of the environmental guidelines given in this handbook appear trivial – mixing your own drink and taking it to work every day instead of buying a can or a carton won't save the planet on its own and does little to combat the threat of climate change or resource depletion. Consider then that in the UK, 24 million drinks are bought every day, most of which are thrown away. Before we campaign on this issue, we must, as individuals, limit our own consumption.

All the environmental damage that is done is done in our name. By taking responsibility for our own lives and the damage we cause ourselves, we can demand that changes are made higher up. By buying products that do less harm, we promote more environmentally acceptable methods of production.

Apply these green guidelines to all aspects of your life, not just those covered in this book. These must be our priorities:

Lowering Energy Consumption – This is a priority if we are to cut down on the amounts of fossil fuels we use and reduce air pollution. Energy efficiency measures in the home are vital, but we also consume fuel indirectly when we buy a new product. An apple shipped all the way from New Zealand has consumed far more than one grown and sold locally. Reducing your indirect energy consumption is as important as lowering how much you use in your home. Reducing energy consumption is also a necessary step if we are to curb further developments in nuclear power.

see Resource Depletion page 33

Reducing Consumption Of Non-renewable Resources – Plastic packaging and many of the products we buy and use, as well as the energy consumed by us and during a product's manufacture, all use up the planet's finite resources. The wasteful way we manufacture and use products in our throwaway society is denying future generations the world's riches which we will have consumed in practically one human generation. In all that you do, reduce, reuse and recycle the resources that support your lifestyle.

Cutting Down Pollution – Buy and use products which have as little an adverse affect on the environment as possible. This includes pollution caused during manufacture, use *and* disposal. It is hard to always make the best choice, or even be aware of the environmental impact of everything that you buy or do, but bear the environment in mind when making difficult choices.

see pages 20, 28 and 34

Reduce Your Own Environmental Exposure – From exhaust fumes to chemicals in food packaging, the human body is being continually bombarded with toxins. Cancers and other diseases are on the increase and already wildlife around the world is paying a heavy toll for our chemical based lifestyle. Stop surrounding yourself and your family with artificial compounds by slowly phasing them out from your home. Natural fibre fabrics, natural dyes for paints and bedclothes, and minimal packaging all benefit you and the environment.

see pages 74, 92 and 96

The environmental threat is still with us. Despite many years of environmental campaigning, progress in some areas has been marred by decline in others. The common thread running through this book is that there is much that has to be done on an individual level in all of our homes to lower the environmental impact of our lives.

see page 36

This Green Home Handbook is only the start.

The Basics

Basic Equipment for a Greener Home

What are the basics necessary to start making your home greener? Getting hold of these basic essentials makes following the suggestions in the handbook easier.

Four million plastic cups are recycled every week in the UK, only a fraction of the number ending up in landfill sites or incinerated.

Vacuum Flask – You can use this for soup as well as tea and coffee. Taking a flask with you to work or on journeys avoids plastic cups, as well as saving money. A jug flask keeps fresh coffee hot, rather than leaving the coffee machine on for long periods.

Eight billion drinks cans are used every year in the UK, less than a quarter are recycled.

Re-Usable Plastic Bottle – Instead of buying individual cans or cartons of juice, buy a bottle of concentrate and mix your own. This saves packaging and money and if the juice comes in a glass bottle, it can be recycled. Cartons are not recyclable in Scotland and few facilities exist for recycling plastic.

Map of Local Bus Routes and Times – If you have a car, the chances are you won't know about your local buses. This is often the main reason people drive even short distances when a bus could take them just as easily. Try to make as many trips by public transport as you can. Some regular trips you could always do by bus.

see Cloth Bags 109

Cloth Shopping Bags – It is hard to get figures for the number of plastic carrier bags given away by supermarkets and shops every day of the week, but the total is in the millions. Taking cloth shopping bags out with you, and refusing carrier bags in shops eliminates the need for plastic bags. You can buy cloth bags in different sizes. They are easily washed and because they are stronger than plastic, they won't rip on the way home with the shopping. Keep cloth bags in handy locations - in your desk at work, in your handbag or on a hook by the front door.

see PVCs page 31

Lunch Box – Making your own packed lunch avoids buying overpackaged and overpriced food. Never wrap your sandwiches in plastic PVC clingfilm. Apart from the environmental dangers of PVC and the waste of resources, dangerous chlorine toxins can leach into your food, especially cheese and other fatty foods. Instead of clingfilm, either don't wrap the sandwiches at all, or use empty bread bags (several times) or brown paper bags. PVC-free clingfilm is available, but is still a waste of plastic.

Basic Cookery Book – Everyone should know how to cook basic meals, but this is not always the case. Cooking food from fresh ingredients saves money and resources - especially packaging. Cooking your own food also means that you can be sure exactly what ingredients you are using, avoiding artificial ingredients and other additives you might want to avoid.

see Greener Cleaning pages 48-50

Washing Soda Crystals – There are many 'eco-friendly' detergents around, but soda crystals are the most economical (70 pence for a kilogram box) and the most versatile way of cleaning your home. Mix them with water and use them for floors, sinks, woodwork, paintwork, drains, washing up, in the washing machine, in the dishwasher and elsewhere around your home.

see page 116

Green Mail Order Catalogues – Many green products are mainly available by mail order from catalogues. Further details are listed in the directory and are correct at the time of going to press. Most of the catalogues are available free - we recommend you send off for them right away. The number to ring for the Friends of the Earth catalogue, which sells everything from tooth brushes with replaceable heads to unbleached cotton dressing gowns, is 01225 442288.

Why Bother?

Throughout this book, Friends of the Earth gives advice on what you should do to cut down the environmental impact of where and how you live. If everybody followed this advice it would have a dramatic impact.

If we are serious about making our society more sustainable, then the first thing that has to change is ourselves. How can we expect huge manufacturing industries to stop belching fumes into the air and causing acid rain, if we are still pouring bleach into the sink, just to get rid of a few tea stains?

If anything is going to change then it has to start with individuals – everything that has changed in the past did so because individuals made it happen, for better or for worse. Milk is still sold in returnable bottles but fewer and fewer people buy it: instead they buy it cheaper from supermarkets and shops, making bottled milk more expensive and perhaps soon to disappear from many areas altogether. If doorstep milk deliveries do vanish in this country, it will be because we'll have stopped buying it, even though glass bottles are far greener than plastic bottles and cartons.

The smallest gestures matter - an American burger chain shortened the length of its drinking straws, saving 500 tonnes of plastic waste a year.

Individuals stopped buying aerosol cans containing ozone-damaging CFCs long before the CFCs were banned and the miraculous fact that the recycling rate in this country is even as high as it is is due almost entirely to individuals saving their recyclables and taking them to the bottle, can and paper banks themselves, unlike in most of Northern Europe where everything is collected from the doorstep. All individual change is crucial and every bit counts. If you won't do anything, then who else will?

Problems and Guilt Trips

You would be forgiven for thinking that the entire 'system' is stacked against people who want to make their homes greener and lead more environmentally-friendly lives, and you could argue that the system itself has got us into this state in the first place. Changes may be difficult to make, greener goods may be hard to find or more expensive. On some occasions you simply won't know the best choice to make; at other times you will have to choose the least green option. But don't give up.

Environmental Quandary – My local shop sells organic milk. I really want to buy it, but it comes all the way from Devon. Surely the pollution from transporting it to Scotland and the energy this consumes cancels out the ecological benefits of it being organic? Ideally, you should buy milk locally, organically and in glass bottles. Until you find this perfect combination, you will have to make compromises. Farmers in Scotland will not produce organic milk unless they are convinced there is a market. Thousands of litres of Devonshire organic milk being sold in Scotland would prove there was demand. Buying organic produce encourages producers to go organic, and shops to sell more organic products.

The Environmental Guilt Trip – The environment takes a battering at Easter and Christmas. I want to have a good time and I don't want my kids to feel left out. What about all those useless and unwanted Christmas presents and the overpackaged (and unhealthy) Easter eggs? Christmas, Easter and other similar events aren't the problem. It's how we celebrate them that causes problems of waste and overconsumption. However, you shouldn't feel that taking environmental issues seriously means having to give up everything you enjoy.

It's Too Expensive – The price we pay rarely reflects the true cost of a product. In any case how do you put a price on the environmental damage caused by shipping fruit half way across the world, or by mining aluminium for disposable drinks cans? The true cost of cheap coffee or clothes may be employees in Third World countries being paid a pittance for a day's work. Closer to home, think of the packaging and other waste we throw out each day to end up in landfill sites. The people who live nearby pay a daily price for what everyone throws out without thinking. It is up to you to decide whether the price is worth paying.

What is a green product?

No product is completely 'environmentally friendly' or 'green'. The biodegradable cleaning product you buy in a supermarket has been transported long distance in a juggernaut. All products consume and pollute somewhere along the line. The solution is to buy products whose environmental impact is as low as possible. Instead of looking for *green* products, we should be buying *greener* products. Make the following your green criteria.

Eight million tonnes of packaging are sold in the UK every year. Of every £50 you spend on your weekly shopping, £8 is spent on packaging.

Minimally Packaged – Look for products without excess packaging. Avoid bottles inside boxes, potatoes in polystyrene trays, shrink-wrapped vegetables or multipacks wrapped in bigger packs. Avoid staple foods, such as rice, sold in excess packaging at higher prices. Try to buy products in recyclable containers – glass, tins, refillable bottles (e.g. detergents and washing up liquid from health food shops) and paper. Large fruits and vegetables, such as melons and cabbages, don't need to be packed in plastic bags.

Made and Sold Locally – Whenever you can, buy products made locally. Freshly-baked bread or cakes are better than pre-packed produce. Meat from the butcher is better than frozen or packaged cuts from the supermarket. Buying or ordering direct from a farmer or local manufacturer reduces packaging and transport and helps your local economy.

Easy to Repair and Made to Last – Buy products which are made to last or can be repaired. Traditional wind-up watches last longer than disposable ones and can be mended. Cheap watches need batteries and are usually not reparable. Second-hand furniture is often more robust than modern self-assembly furniture. Avoid replacing something simply because it looks out of date or old fashioned. Find out whether spare parts are available for broken equipment, such as a new glass jug for your coffee machine.

In France, for £6, you can buy five disposable T-shirts designed to be worn once and then thrown away.

Non-Disposable – More and more products are specifically designed to be thrown away after use. Disposable cutlery, plates, cups and pens were followed by disposable nappies, throw-away cameras and now contact lenses. Don't buy items designed to be thrown away. Instead of a paper tablecloth, buy one you can wash or wipe.

Energy Efficient – An alarm clock uses no energy once it has been manufactured, apart from the energy you use to wind it up at night. A clock radio has to be permanently plugged in, simply to wake you up in the morning. Although the energy consumed by one clock radio is fairly insignificant, when you add up the number of televisions, radios, videos and hi-fis left permanently on standby, the total energy consumption starts to become significant. Avoid equipment which needlessly consumes power, e.g. electric toothbrush or electric can opener. Whatever you buy, check its energy consumption.

Only as Small as You Need – Don't buy a large item for a task which could be done by a smaller version. An extra-large tin-opener, for instance, will have the same working parts as a smaller one, but it will cost twice as much and be made out of three times the amount of metal and plastic. The only time bigger is better is when the product lasts twice as long, saving resources in the long run.

Non-Polluting – Most manufactured products will have caused some kind of pollution before arriving in your house - through resource extraction, the manufacturing process, packaging or transportation. Many products pollute you and your home by emitting toxins and consume energy during their use. If they are not recycled, they pollute during disposal. Different products pollute more at different stages of their life cycles. Try to limit the impact on yourself and the environment.

see page 16

Eco-Label – Labels and logos on products attesting to their performance on environmental or other criteria have a dubious reputation in this country. Many labels have no scientific substance but are simply advertising gimmicks cashing in on green awareness. Even seemingly trustworthy descriptions such as 'recyclable' or 'biodegradable' are totally meaningless without proper justification. To end the confusion, and to help consumers make ethical choices, properly authenticated labels are being set up by responsible bodies. The principal eco-label, being set up across the European Union is the official EU Eco-Label.

Environmental Labels

With the emergence of green consumerism, companies saw opportunities to cash in on raised public awareness. Products began to appear with labels or logos making all sorts of claims about environmental performance. These logos endorsed products as 'environmentally-friendly' or biodegradable, without any evidence or proof to back up such claims. With no legal backing to these claims, the legitimate attempts by companies to sell products on the basis of genuine environmental performance were undermined. Other countries have national eco-labels which consumers can trust. They know that by choosing a product with an eco-label, they are making the best choice as far as the environment is concerned.

European Eco-Label (all products) – This label is still being developed for eventual use on consumer products throughout the EU. Currently, only a few products have been through trials but as the scheme develops, more products will be eligible. The EU Eco-Label will become the main European label describing environmental performance.

Three Arrows (all products) – This common label is generally understood by the public to mean recycled. In reality, however, the label is meaningless. It can mean a product is made of 10% or 100% recycled material. It is often used to mean *recyclable* rather than recycled, which means nothing unless the product is actually recycled. The label can add unwarranted kudos to a product. For instance, many plastics can be recycled but the facilities are not generally available in Scotland.

The Blue Angel Mark (all products) – This successful and respected German label is used on a wide variety of products. It sets extremely tough environmental standards to which products must adhere to qualify. Although the Blue Angel is German, any company can apply to join the scheme, so you will find it on products on sale in this country.

The Nordic Swan (paper) – This label describes emissions during the paper production process. It does not refer to other features such as the recycled content. Paper mills have to reach minimum performance standards in five different categories before they can be considered for the award. Originally the Nordic Swan was only given to paper mills in Scandinavia, but the awarding body will now consider applications from elsewhere in Europe. Look for it on envelopes and stationery.

Der Grüne Punkt (The Green Point) (all products) – *Beware*, this is not an environmental label and is only valid in France and Germany. A product bearing a Grüne Punkt means only that the manufacturers have contributed towards the cost of collecting and recycling that product's packaging in France and Germany. In Scotland, the label is meaningless, and even in France and Germany it only means that the packaging will be collected for recycling and says nothing about the environmental performance of the product.

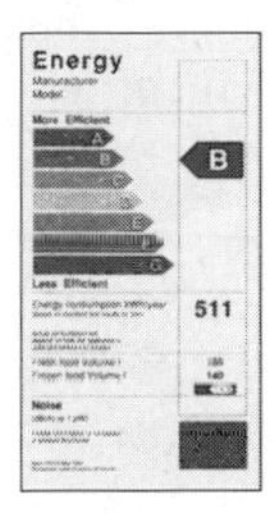

EU Energy Label (domestic electric appliances) – This new European label provides information on a product's energy consumption and operating noise. Fridges, freezers, washing machines and tumble dryers are legally required to carry the label and other products should soon follow. It allows easy comparison between different makes and models.

see Timber page 103

The Forest Stewardship Council Certification Mark (timber and wood products) – The FSC mark is new in the UK. It certifies that the source of wood or timber is an accredited forest managed according to the guidelines of the International Forest Stewardship Council, of which Friends of the Earth is a member. Look for the mark on wood products such as doors, shelves and timber in DIY shops. Ask for it if you can't find it.

see Fairtrade page 42

The Fairtrade Mark (mostly food products) – The Fairtrade Mark is run by the Fairtrade Foundation, a charity set up by organisations including Oxfam and Christian Aid. The aim of the Fairtrade Foundation is to help alleviate poverty in developing countries by guaranteeing that producers and workers earn fair wages, and have decent working and housing conditions. The Fairtrade Foundation also ensures that products bearing the mark meet established environmental standards. By buying products bearing this mark, you can be sure that the profits go direct to the producer rather than to middle men and large multinational companies. These products are available in health food and charity shops, but gradually they are appearing in supermarkets.

The Freedom Food Label (meat products) – The Freedom Food label is administered by the RSPCA and ensures that farm animals used in food production enjoy 'five freedoms': freedom from fear and distress, freedom from pain, injury and disease, freedom from hunger and thirst, freedom from discomfort and freedom to express normal behaviour. These freedoms must apply throughout an animal's life, including during transport and slaughter.

The Soil Association Organic Standard (food products) – This symbol operates under European law and guarantees that a product conforms to EU standards of organic farming. Because these standards are European, ingredients and products from abroad are also guaranteed organic. The symbol applies to all types of food and agriculture, including animal products and items such as bread, spreads and prepared meals.

Environmental Issues

Air Pollution

Air pollution kills many thousands of people in the UK each year. It affects the health of many more and costs the country billions of pounds in NHS bills, lost productivity, reduced crop yields and damage to buildings. Air pollution is also responsible for acid rain and climate change.

Air pollutants are usually present in very small quantities but even at low levels they can have serious effects on people and the environment. Different pollutants act in different ways, and their combined effects are often severe. The main pollutants are:

Carbon Dioxide (CO_2) – This gas comes mainly from burning fossil fuels and contributes to global climate change.

Nitrogen Dioxide (NO_2) – This comes mainly from traffic. It exacerbates respiratory problems and contributes to acid rain, low level ozone and smog.

Carbon Monoxide (CO) – This comes mainly from traffic (also faulty gas appliances), and causes drowsiness, headaches, impaired brain function and death.

Benzene and other Volatile Organic Compounds (VOCs) – These are mainly emitted by fuels and industrial processes. Benzene causes cancer. Other organic compunds contribute to global climate change and ground-level ozone.

Polycyclic Aromatic Hydrocarbons (PAHs) – These come mainly from traffic and coal burning. Some are carcinogenic.

Ozone (O_3) – This is caused by sunlight reacting with nitrogen dioxide and other pollutants. Although useful in the upper atmosphere, at ground level ozone causes irritation to eyes, nose and throat, lung inflammation and possibly cancer. It also damages plants and reduces crop yields.

Sulphur Dioxide (SO_2) – This comes mainly from burning fossil fuels. It can cause serious breathing difficulties, has a toxic effect on plants, damages stonework and metals and is the major cause of acid rain.

Particulate Matter (PM) – This is a complex mix of small particles of both liquids and solids. In cities the main source is normally traffic, especially diesel vehicles. It is responsible for many deaths each year.

Lead and other metals – These are in the air and come from road transport, metal production processes and coal burning.

Transport – Most pollution comes from the transport sector, particularly road traffic. Although tightening standards will reduce emissions from individual vehicles, the projected increase in vehicle ownership will soon outstrip these improvements. Transport is also the sector with the fastest rising contribution to CO_2 emissions and climate change.

The problems caused by air pollution are not equally distributed. Those most at risk contribute least to the problem – the young, the infirm and the elderly. These groups are also likely to have least control over their exposure, e.g. by moving house to less polluted areas.

Pollution by particulates costs Scotland around £1.5bn a year.

Health – The Government has estimated that the health of as many as 1 in 3 people in the UK may be at risk from the air they breathe. The number of asthma cases has risen dramatically. Hospital admissions in Scotland have doubled in the past 10 years and the condition kills around 2,000 people in the UK every year. This is partially attributed to air pollution. Particulates have now been shown to have extremely serious health effects causing around 1100 deaths a year in Scotland alone. Even if new standards are met, a 3-day particulate air pollution episode, could kill10 Scots, send another 15 to hospital and make 3000 asthmatics reach for their inhalers.

Crop yields and forest production may be reduced by as much as 10%.

Environment – Acid rain damages trees, wildlife, lochs and buildings. A United Nations survey in 1988 found UK tree damage second only to Czechoslovakia. 20-30 Scottish lochs are now fishless. At the same time, ground-level ozone impedes plant and tree growth and climate change threatens widespread disruption of many natural systems.

Ozone damage to buildings and materials costs Scotland £50m annually.

Climate Change

Scientific opinion is now united that the planet is facing an unprecedented period of climate change. Initially, this means a warming of the atmosphere leading to storms, rising sea levels, droughts and the spread of disease. Long term predictions are that as the entire climatic system is upset, the knock-on effects will mean some parts of the planet enduring ice-age conditions whilst others bake.

The Greenhouse Effect – Naturally occurring gases in the atmosphere, mainly water vapour and carbon dioxide, trap heat from the Sun, keeping the Earth around 30°C warmer than it would otherwise be. Without these 'greenhouse gases', the Earth's surface would be frozen and lifeless. The atmosphere is normally self regulating, a complicated interrelationship between it and the surface of the planet – the forests and the oceans. Many millions of tonnes of CO_2, for example, are locked up in the world's forests and oceans, in rocks such as chalk, and in oil and coal reserves. Burning oil and coal, and felling the forests without replacing them, releases the carbon dioxide that the planet has stored over millions of years back into the atmosphere faster than the planet can re-absorb it.

The natural balance between the various gases in the atmosphere is being drastically altered by our industrial activities.

The average July temperature in Inverness is predicted to be just 9°C (49°F), with an average January temperature in Edinburgh of -1°C (30°F).

Climate Change – The Earth is already 0.5°C warmer than in 1900, and scientists predict a further increase of 0.5-2°C even without reducing current pollution levels. If we carry on polluting at current rates we can expect a further warming of 0.8-3.5°C. If this doesn't sound like much, consider the fact that there are only a couple of degrees of difference between the temperature now and during the last Ice Age.

A major implication for Scotland is that the Gulf Stream, which keeps the British Isles 5% warmer than we would otherwise be during the winter months, will weaken and ultimately vanish. The Gulf Stream is produced by a complex set of deep water currents and wind patterns which will be upset by climate changes. The Odden Feature, a tongue of ice which forms off the coast of Greenland each winter, and which is one of the Gulf Stream's major 'pumps', has been missing since 1994. The Gulf Stream has disappeared in the past, particularly during the ice ages, and evidence in the Arctic ice suggests that this can happen very rapidly.

The major human contributions to climate change are carbon dioxide, methane, nitrous dioxide and a range of artificial industrial chemicals such as CFCs and HFCs. Carbon dioxide (CO_2) stays in the atmosphere for approximately 120 years, making it a very potent greenhouse gas. It is our main pollutant as far as climate change is concerned, and is caused mainly by transport and the burning of coal and other fossil fuels for electricity. Electricity generation accounts for 21% of Scotland's CO_2 emissions. Other gases are far more powerful as greenhouse gases. A sulphur hexafluoride (SF6) molecule for instance has a global warming potential 25,000 times greater than a single CO_2 molecule, so although there is only a small amount of this gas in the atmosphere, its impact is huge. SF6 is used as an insulating gas in the electricity industry – its atmospheric concentration is growing by 8% a year and yet it is not even mentioned in the government's climate change strategy.

see Human Health page 35

Human Health – As the climate is disrupted, changeable weather will seriously threaten agriculture and human health. Certain areas will suffer extreme drought, notably Africa and Southern Europe, and wetter warmer weather moving further north will bring with it diseases such as malaria. If the climate changes faster than natural vegetation can adapt, changes in rainfall distribution may result in severe soil erosion, threatening agriculture. World food reserves will be endangered as grain harvests fail in the planet's major growing areas, making it difficult to feed a global population of 12 billion people by 2100.

Renewable Energy

Unlike oil, gas, coal and even nuclear power, which uses uranium, renewable energy sources (wind, water, solar) will never run out. Renewable energy does not pollute on anything like the scale that burning fossil fuels does. It is far cheaper than nuclear power and infinitely safer. Renewable energy is vital if we are to move to a sustainable and less environmentally-damaging society because a society which depends on polluting, dangerous and declining sources of power is ultimately unsustainable. Sooner or later, alternative energy sources must be used.

The biggest obstacle to renewable energy production is economics. Political decisions ensure that the vast bulk of research funding in this country goes to the nuclear industry, making investment in cheap and clean energy extremely difficult. However, the potential for renewable energy is huge, and gradually wind farms and other projects are appearing across the country.

Wind Power – There are currently three wind farms in Scotland – Hagshaw Hill in Lanarkshire, Windy Standard in Kirkcudbrightshire and Nova in Easter Ross. Approximately 14% of homes in Lanarkshire are supplied by wind power. There are over 30 windfarms in the UK, including the largest in Europe in Powys, Wales. Across the country there are also many individual turbines, either supplying small areas or powering individual houses or buildings, particularly in rural areas, and places not on the grid.

Scotland has 40% of Europe's wind capacity.

Opponents of wind power argue that windmills are noisy, intrusive and blots on the landscape. Many of these objections can be overcome by sensible site selection and modern windmills are designed to be as silent as possible. Many people consider windmills to be attractive and deeply symbolic of clean technology, making the debate a subjective rather than scientific one. Given the windy expanse of ocean around Scotland, there is enormous potential for off-shore wind farms, as exist already in Denmark and Norway. One such wind farm is proposed for the coast of Norfolk.

Windmills use very little land. Although a wind farm may be spread over a large area, 98% of the land beneath can still be used for agriculture and when turbines are dismantled, they leave no trace.

Compare this with the reactor of a nuclear power station which must be entombed, remaining radioactive for 250 000 years.

In 1995, the Department of Trade and Industry invested £500 000 in solar power compared to £22 million in nuclear power.

Solar Power – Despite our climate, there is great potential for solar power in Scotland, particularly in the summer when we receive as much as 60% of the amount of sunshine hitting the equator. Since our homes need the heating on for longer than those further south, the savings to be made are even greater. Solar power channels heat and light from the Sun. At Strathclyde University, a student residence was constructed using transparent insulating material which lets in and stores heat from the Sun. Even in the middle of winter almost no heating is required to maintain the internal temperature at 23°C. Incorporating such 'passive' solar features into the design of new buildings is a cost-effective way of reducing energy consumption.

Photovoltaic cells convert the energy of the sun into electricity and are usually found in solar panels. As technology advances, solar panels will become more efficient and cheaper. Warmer countries, such as Israel, generate a vast proportion of their domestic electricity through rooftop solar panels, whilst places such as California have huge solar panel farms in the desert.

Hydro Power – The most well-developed form of renewable energy, hydro power supplies Scotland with 10% of its electricity. Larger hydro power schemes rely on reservoirs and dams to be built to guarantee a continual flow of water, but smaller scale projects also exist. Scotland's natural geography and microclimate mean hydro power could be a greater future source of electricity.

Other types of renewable power include wave, tidal and geothermal power, all of which have the potential for further development in Scotland. There is no single solution to the problem of energy generation. Instead a combined approach, which stresses energy efficiency to reduce energy demand along with the use of renewable sources, is needed.

Transport

In the last 40 years, traffic volumes in Britain have increased six fold and this trend is set to continue. The rise is due to a number of factors including increased car ownership and a growth in the overall number and length of journeys. This shift towards the private car has been exacerbated by car travel becoming cheaper in comparison to public transport.

Only 6% of freight in the UK goes by rail

Transport and Air Pollution – Motor vehicle exhaust emissions have now overtaken industry as the major source of air pollution in Britain. Transport is responsible for 31% of Scotland's carbon dioxide emissions, compared to 25% for industry. Recent surveys show that Scottish cities suffer from severe air pollution, consistently exceeding EU guidelines for air quality. A 1995 government survey showed that Glasgow's Hope Street had the joint worst air pollution in the UK.

Transport and Energy – Land transport accounts for a quarter of the UK's total fuel energy use, more than either domestic or industrial consumption. Transport's share of fuel consumption has grown over the past ten years with the increase in traffic volumes. Conservation of non-renewable oil reserves is therefore, in itself, a major imperative for reducing traffic levels.

Road-building and Aggregates – A third of Britain's production of aggregates (sand, gravel and broken stone) is used to build and maintain roads. The Government forecasts that demand for aggregates will double over the next 20 years because of the road-building programme. This demand will mean increased mining and quarrying with more proposals such as the recent Harris 'superquarry' with potentially devastating effects on the local environment and communities.

Road-building itself is becoming increasingly unacceptable, both at a local and national level. Locally, new roads often cut through natural areas containing important wildlife and archaeological features as well as local amenity sites. Where new roads go through urban areas (such as the M77 and M74 extensions in Glasgow) they blight local communities with extra noise and pollution. New roads, rather than relieving congestion, create 'induced' traffic by bringing more places within easy driving distance, adding extra traffic to existing levels. All new road building therefore has national implications of extra air pollution and energy consumption.

Transport and Congestion – In addition to the economic costs of congestion, estimated at £21 billion a year by the CBI, an increasingly car-dominated society undermines quality of life. Those without cars and dependent on a declining and expensive public transport system, particularly the young, the elderly and women with children, find life increasingly difficult as services and public transport vanish in car-based areas. Cars encourage out-of-town supermarkets, condemning local community shopping centres, and as traffic increases, so it becomes more dangerous for children to walk to school, curtailing their independence and freedom.

Although the number has fallen over the past 60 years, ten road-related deaths per day is still too high. Whether you have a car or not, it is hard to dispute that we are in need of a change to a more integrated and less environmentally-damaging method of transport.

Percentage of journeys made by bike:

In Europe	
Netherlands	29%
Denmark	18.4%
Finland (winter)	12.3%
Germany	11%
Britain	2.3%
In Britain	
York	15.7%
Hull	11.5%
Southampton	3.7%
Nottingham	2.5%
Liverpool	1.4%
Edinburgh	1.5%
Glasgow	0.6%

Transport Policy – There needs to be a major shift in transport policy away from road-building and the private car towards a more balanced approach. This would encourage a mixture of choices incorporating public transport, cycling and walking as well as actually reducing the need to travel in the first place. Over half of all journeys made are under five miles, ideal for being cycled. Other northern European countries with similar climates have much higher cycling rates than ours mainly because of different cultural attitudes towards cycling and strong government encouragement for cycle facilities. Bus and rail transport needs investment to increase reliability and efficiency to become a real alternative to the car. Town and city centres need to become more pedestrian friendly, with far more pedestrianisation than is currently the case, while shops and services need to be built, located and developed near the communities they serve.

Waste Disposal

95% of Scotland's waste is dumped in the ground in landfill sites where it will remain forever. A small but significant proportion of the remaining waste is incinerated. The potential for recycling is huge.

The average family throws away around one tonne of waste every year.

Landfill Sites – Dumping creates a variety of problems. Liquids from decomposing rubbish, such as acids from batteries, and rainfall react together to produce toxic solutions which leach out, polluting rivers, underground water as well as the soil itself, eventually penetrating the food chain. Decomposing rubbish produces methane gas, which is both dangerous at a local level and a greenhouse gas 20 times more powerful than carbon dioxide.

Landfilling creates physical problems. The sites are ugly blots on the landscape spreading litter to surrounding areas. They attract rodents and other pests, and require continuous lorry shipments in and out of the plant, with associated problems of dust, noise and air pollution.

Until recently, landfilling was a cheap option with Scotland having a plentiful supply of suitable sites, mainly abandoned quarries. The low costs involved meant there was no real economic incentive for local authorities, or any other body, to seriously address waste reduction and recycling. The Government has now introduced a landfill tax of £7 per tonne of waste. This means that costs will increase, creating a financial as well as an environmental reason for recycling. Through recycling local authorities will be able to *make* savings.

Waste Incineration – Burning waste is increasingly seen as a convenient way of dealing with waste disposal, particularly when combined with electricity generation. However this process is both polluting and inefficient.

Strictly speaking, incineration cannot be classified as waste disposal because burning waste simply reduces its volume by two thirds, leaving large quantities of ash still for disposal. Since burning waste material alters its chemical composition, the remaining incinerator waste is highly toxic. When added to landfill sites this leaches into the environment. Particularly toxic items of waste such as batteries and PVC plastics leave ash full of dioxins and other toxic chemicals.

Incinerators create air pollution. Cadmium, mercury, nitrogen oxide, sulphur dioxide and hydrogen chloride are all released into the atmosphere, damaging trees, crops, human health and creating acid rain. This atmospheric pollution can be reduced by cleaning or 'scrubbing' the output from incinerators, but this leaves a different type of toxic waste which needs further treatment. 'Wet scrubbing', for instance, produces toxic sludge where once there was recyclable plastic. Apart from the pollution they cause, incinerators are extremely inefficient at converting heat from burning waste into energy, producing far less than would be saved by recycling, making this a very wasteful way of producing energy.

see Recycling page 30

This, coupled with the fact that by burning materials such as plastic we waste a resource that could be continually recycled, makes incineration a wasteful and inefficient way of dealing with our rubbish.

Biodegradable – Not everything that is biodegradable gets the chance to do so in landfill sites. Decomposition requires specific conditions, including air, which vast uncontrolled landfill sites cannot provide. Unlike proper composting, whose end product is soil, anything which rots down in landfill sites is so contaminated by plastics, metals and dangerous chemicals that nothing can be done with it.

As well as creating pollution, dumping and burning is a tragic waste of the world's resources. The amount of waste we create in the first place has to be reduced, before the next step is taken, that of recycling what we do throw out.

Recycling

The average dustbin contains:

paper and card	33%
glass	10%
plastic	7%
ferrous metal	7%
textile	4%
aluminium, cans and foil	1%
compost material, dust and ash	38%

Saving Resources – Steel, aluminium and plastic are all precious resources. They are all derivatives of raw materials originally mined from the earth and being depleted at an alarming rate. Paper, too, is a valuable resource whose raw material (trees) is being consumed faster than it is being renewed. Glass is made from sand, which has to be extracted and processed. When we throw things away, we deprive future generations of the resources we take for granted. We are literally 'wasting' resources forever.

Any product made from recycled material saves resources. The rarer the material, or the more environmentally-damaging it is to produce, the greater the environmental savings. Aluminium, for instance, is made from bauxite – 4 tonnes of which are needed to make 1 tonne of aluminium. The mining process itself damages the local ecology, decimating landscapes and causing high levels of pollution. The process uses large quantities of water, leaving rivers and streams badly silted up. The processing of bauxite into aluminium requires vast amounts of energy and produces a great deal of waste to be disposed of. Aluminium is almost 100% recyclable, cutting down the need to mine new bauxite and its attendant problems.

Energy savings from using recycled rather than virgin material:

aluminium cans	96%
copper	88-95%
glass	22%
lead	65%
nickel	95%
paper	70%
polyethylene	97%
rubber	70%
steel and iron	74%

Saving Energy – It takes less energy to recycle materials into new products than to make the same product from virgin material. Manufacturing one aluminium drinks can uses up the equivalent of half a can of oil. Recycling the can requires only six percent of the energy used in its original manufacture. Making paper from recycled fibres uses much less energy and resources than making it from virgin wood pulp. Recycling your household waste adds significantly to the energy savings you can make in your home.

Reducing Waste – All non-recycled waste has to be dealt with somehow, often to the detriment of the local environment. The more waste is recycled, the less has to be landfilled.

see Recycling page 112

Buying Recycled – There is no point taking your waste to be recycled if you don't also buy products made from recycled materials. Economics is a major obstacle to greater recycling – it is still cheaper for companies to use virgin instead of recycled materials. Increased public demand will drive down costs

PVC: A Deadly Plastic

PVC – Polyvinyl chloride is a plastic containing the the deadly chemical chloride. PVC pollutes the environment throughout its entire life cycle and at some point the toxic chemicals will end up back in the environment. In addition, PVC production requires huge amounts of energy.

PVC for drinks packaging is banned in Switzerland

PVC is used for packaging in cling film, bottles and vacuum packs. It is used in the building industry to make window frames, plastic panelling, pipes, gutters and cables, and in home decorating for flooring, wallpaper, blinds and shower curtains. It is also used to make pens, credit cards and toys.

see Gender Benders page 74

Production of PVC – When PVC is manufactured, dioxins are created and released. Dioxins are highly toxic and are associated with immune system problems and cancer. They are potential hormone disrupters. PVCs contain phthalates to make the plastic more flexible. 95% of all phthalates are made for the production of PVC. Using PVC as packaging poses the risk of having pollutants and chemicals leach into food and drinks.

Disposal – PVC causes more environmental problems during disposal. When incinerated, it releases toxins and gases which must be treated. It also leaves highly-polluted ash which mixes with water and other chemicals to form a highly-toxic liquid which can leak into the surrounding water table. Even landfilling un-incinerated PVC poses similar problems. Recycling PVC is difficult and results in more toxic emissions. Even recycled plastic must ultimately be disposed of.

Alternatives – There are many alternatives to PVC. Choose glass, paper and card rather than plastic packaging. Where you have to choose plastic, look for alternatives to PVC, such as PET, polypropylene (PP) and polyethylene (PE). Alternatives to PVC are used far more widely in other parts of Europe than in the UK, showing the potential for change in this country. On all plastic products and packaging, a number inside a triangle identifies which type of plastic it is. PVC is number 3.

Packaging: The Environmental Connection

Most packaging is made of plastic, which is in turn made from oil, a non-renewable resource. The rest is made of tin, aluminium, glass, paper and cardboard. Convenience packaging means products can be sold anywhere in the world, often thousands of miles away from the point of production. This means more transport and more pollution.

Most packaging is designed to be disposable - consuming vast amounts of energy and resources for a life that sometimes lasts just a few hours. The cardboard box for a take-away pizza costs 20 pence, and the pizza is eaten within half an hour of being bought. A plastic bottle of milk will only be used once before being thrown away whilst the average glass milk bottle is used around 40 times.

Whereas in Scotland only a fraction of packaging is recycled, other European countries set strict quotas for how much *cannot* be recycled. Many countries emphasise returnable and refillable packaging before recycling so products are sold in durable containers that get used time and time again.

Apply the three Rs hierarchy when shopping:

Reduce – Limit the packaging you buy. Choose products that are simply packaged. Buy in bulk so you get proportionally less packaging in ratio to the weight of what you buy. Health food and mail order companies sell some items, such as tea, rice and detergents in bulk. This is also cheaper.

Reuse/Refill – Buy products in refillable or reusable packaging whenever you can. Health food shops sell detergents in re-fillable bottles; some soft drinks companies in Scotland still use deposit bottles and milk bottle deliveries are still made in much of the country.

This Swedish fruit juice bottle is sold with a deposit, and is refillable.

Recycle – When the above two options have run out, recycle what is left. This means buying packaging that is recyclable - glass, card and tin instead of plastic. Make sure you do then recycle it.

Resource Depletion

Consumption of Non-Renewable Resources – As the population grows and we consume and produce increasing quantities, we use up the planet's finite resources – non-renewable resources which can never be replaced. These are fossil fuels (oil, coal and gas) which povide most of our energy and materials such as plastic. We also consume large amounts of steel, aluminium, lead and copper. Reserves of oil, gas and coal are particularly limited – extractable oil reserves off the coast of Scotland are estimated to run out within twenty years.

Although new technology allows more inaccessible oil and coal to be extracted and new deposits are still being discovered, it is fair to say that one in one human lifetime, almost all of the world's supply of fossil fuels, built up over millions of years, will have been exhausted.

For the Chinese to have the same number of cars per person as Taiwan, the planet will have to find enough raw materials for 182 milllion cars. Japan produces 5 million cars a year.

Population Growth – In 1850 the Earth's population stood at one billion. By 1987 it numbered five billion, reaching 6 billion by the turn of the century, doubling to 12 billion within another 80 years. Before the 1800s the global population had remained constant for many thousands of years. Now we and the planet are faced with the unprecedented prospect of many billions of new humans to support using rapidly-dwindling resources. The fastest increases in population are taking place in developing countries where rising living standards are leading to higher material expectations.

Western countries use far more resources than poorer and less industrialised ones. North America, for instance, produces twice as much electricity each year as South America and, with 6% of the world population, owns 37% of the world's motor vehicles. With the global population set to reach 12 billion by the middle of the next century, pressure on the planet's resources can only increase.

Acid Rain

Acid rain, which includes acid snow and acid mist, is formed when nitrogen dioxide and sulphur oxides combine with water in the atmosphere to form weak sulphuric and nitric acids. In extreme conditions, rain can be as acid as vinegar. Although emissions of sulphur and nitrogen oxides in Scotland are small in relation to other parts of the UK and Europe, acidic emissions in England and the Scottish central belt have had a significant impact on our urban and rural areas.

The UK exports most of its air pollution. A survey in 1990 in southern Norway found that fish had virtually disappeared from lakes and rivers over an 18,000 km^2 area due to acidification of the water. 11% of the total land area of Norway is seriously affected, whilst in Sweden, 14,000 lakes have been acidified, 4,000 severely. 15% of Norway's acid rain comes from the UK, the largest single contributor.

65% of Sites of Special Scientific Interest surveyed in Scotland with standing or running water are affected by acidification of surface waters.

In the UK, the problems are no less severe. 86% of our acid rain comes from domestic sources, with the west coast of Scotland being particularly badly affected through its high rainfall. The sensitive nature of the environment in the western Highlands makes the problem even more acute. 55% of all British oak trees over 60 years old are moderately to severely damaged by acid rain. In 1988, a UN survey found that in Europe, only Czechoslovakia had more damaged trees than Britain.

5-10% of Scottish freshwaters have been reduced to a pH of 5.5 over the past 100 years. Below this level fish populations are seriously damaged and some 20–30 lochs have become fishless. Acid rain also eats away at our architectural heritage. Buildings and key monuments in Glasgow have suffered serious and irreparable damage.

The Ozone Layer

The ozone layer is a thin layer of gas surrounding the planet. It shields the Earth's surface by absorbing much of the Sun's ultraviolet (UV) radiation, particularly the shorter-wavelength radiation, the most harmful to life. Chloroflourocarbons (CFCs), halons and related chemicals all contribute to the destruction of the ozone layer by reacting with ozone gas molecules and splitting them apart. Each CFC molecule can react with many thousands of ozone molecules during its lifetime and it takes several years for CFCs to reach the ozone layer. Even if we were to stop releasing CFCs into the atmosphere today, the damage will continue for another fifty years.

The hole in the ozone layer was first discovered over Antarctica in the early eighties, appearing every spring and lasting the whole summer. Although no hole has yet appeared over the northern hemisphere, ozone levels are thin enough each year to begin causing serious damage. The summer of 1996 saw record lows above northern Europe and the situation is not forecast to improve until the middle of the 21st century.

Human Health – One of the main effects of ozone depletion is an increase in skin cancer and cancers in other parts of the body, such as the salivary gland. Eyes have no protection against UV radiation, making them particularly vulnerable. In the southern hemisphere, catarcacts are become more and more common as are other diseases such as snow blindness. Of particular concern is the fact that UV radiation suppresses the human immune system, lowering our tolerance to diseases, especially those which enter through the skin, such as malaria. UV rays activates HIV in infected people, prompting it to progress into full blown AIDS.

see Human Health
page 23

The Environment – Increases in UV light damage plants directly and make them more prone to disease. Many species of tree come into leaf earlier under higher than normal levels of UV light, making them vulnerable to frosts. Other plants, including crops, are severely affected by increases in UV, particularly when combined with other environmental stresses. In the sea, plankton and algae are damaged by UV radiation. Plankton is an important source of food for the whole marine ecosystem as well as playing an important role in controlling global temperature.

Friends of the Earth Scotland Campaigns

Being a green consumer and making your home as green as possible is one of the most important things you can be doing as an individual, but if you want to take it further there are many opportunities. For changes to be made, pressure must be brought to bear on the Government and industry to make moves in a more sustainable direction. Examples of good practice exist abroad, from the cycle lanes of Amsterdam to returnable bottles in Germany. A major reason that so much green progress is being made in other countries is that the political will for change exists alongside consumer pressure. Here concerted action is vital to campaign for environmental change.

see page 148

Air Pollution and Transport – FoE Scotland campaigns for investment in public transport and a change of priorities away from cars and road building towards clean air in our towns and cities. We have published 'The State of Scotland's Air', the first report looking at the country's air quality. We work closely with other groups in Scotland contributing to a sensible transport policy for the next century. Send off for a fight the fumes pack containing an air monitoring kit for you to monitor your most polluted local street. Join FoE Scotland's annual 'Bike to the Future' sponsored cycle ride – a valuable fundraiser and an effective statement of solidarity for cyclists and would-be cyclists alike.

see Air Pollution page 28
and Transport page 26

Gender-benders – FoE Scotland has carried out its own research into the chemicals in daily use which are affecting the hormone balance in humans and nature. There is only so much an individual can do to avoid these toxic chemicals so the government and industry must do more to take them out of everyday products. Cards listing products to avoid are available for you to carry with you shopping and FoE Scotland is working hard to campaign on this issue.

see Gender Benders
page 74

see page 150

Dounreay Nuclear Facility – The UK's only nuclear establishment to resemble a tea bag – 50,000 perforations and counting. To shut Dounreay has been one of FoE Scotland's long term campaigns as evidence of leaks and malpractice continues to emerge. We have taken on the German, Australian and US governments to stop transports of nuclear waste being sent to Scotland for reprocessing, successfully stopping the shipments from across the Atlantic.

Send off for a campaign pack to help us to shut down this monster and create economic, environmental and social regeneration of the community in the north of Scotland.

see Renewable Energy page 24

Renewable Energy – This is what is needed to tackle the problems created by nuclear power and the over consumption of fossil fuels. FoE Scotland is working together with groups in eight other European countries to develop a renewable energy strategy for Europe. Here in Scotland, we have published guidelines for developers and local communities covering sensitive planning for renewable energy. Send off for our 'Renew Scotland' pack, part of our campaign to promote wind power.

see Waste Disposal page 28

see page 149

Waste and Recycling – FoE campaigns to reduce the amount of packaging in everyday use that is destined for the landfill site. Our 'Pack Back' campaign relies upon individuals sending back to the guilty companies' head offices all the waste packaging they normally expect us to pay for. Help get the message across to the supermarkets and manufacturers, order your 'Pack Back' campaign kit. Other work carried out by FoE Scotland is to continually pressure local authorities to increase recycling and to campaign for more sustainable ways of dealing with waste.

Superquarries – Scotland is facing the growing threat of having some of its most beautiful areas scarred by massive quarries. Friends of the Earth has been involved in opposing the proposed massive Isle of Harris superquarry, which, if it goes ahead, will act as a precedent for equally huge quarries all over Scotland. At the time of going to press, we are awaiting the Government's decision based on the findings of the public inquiry into the proposal. FoE was one of the groups which campaigned to have the inquiry opened in the first place. Help in this campaign by ordering our booklet 'The case against the Harris superquarry'.

see page 148

Use Your Rights – Every day of every year the local environment is under threat – from developers trying to get planning applications through on greenbelt land or someone intending to chop down trees in the local park. Find out your legal rights and demand access to information. FoE Scotland has produced the first ever 'Citizens Guide To Protecting The Environment'. The revised and expanded edition is due out in June 1997.

Shopping For Food

Food is generally a household's biggest single area of expenditure. A Danish survey found that food is a household's single largest contribution to environmental damage. The energy used to cook food is only the tip of the iceberg as far as the environment is concerned.

The ecological impact of food begins when land has to be cleared for agriculture. This may mean felling forests or growing crops on marginal land unsuited to agriculture, needing continual irrigation or fertilising, and leading to irreversible soil erosion. In poorer countries, heavily dependent on unsustainable agricultural crops to export to repay debts, pressure on the land is such that indigenous populations are expelled from the land to make way for cash crops. Between 1960 and 1985, 40% of all Central America's rainforests were cleared for beef pasture. This pattern is replicated across the world.

Over a 25 year period, Ecuador lost 50,000 species through clearing land for banana plantations for export.

Intensive farming depends on large amounts of artificial chemicals, often adding to the human costs of food through exposing workers to toxic chemicals and contamination incidents, as well as polluting the soil and water.

It would take only 13 years to deplete the planet's known petroleum reserves if all the world's food was produced using North American methods.

Transporting, packaging and processing add to food's environmental impact. 'Food miles' describe the distance food travels before reaching our tables. In the US, for example, an average food item travels 1,200 miles before being consumed. A German strawberry yoghurt distributed and sold throughout Europe was made from north German yoghurt, Polish strawberries, Dutch corn and wheat flour, west German jam and east German sugar beet. The aluminium for the lid was manufactured 300km away.

Fruit And Vegetables

Try local organic farm outlets or subscribe to a box scheme, which will deliver a weekly supply of seasonal fruit and vegetables.

see Organic Farms page 128

Until recently, the fruit and vegetables on sale in shops and markets would have told you what the season was. The arrival of summer would have been heralded by the first raspberries, whilst autumn would have meant apples and turnips. Easter, Christmas, Halloween and other traditional feasts and festivals used the fruits of the season. Yet nowadays, the same range of fruit and vegetables is available all year round.

Prices may vary slightly according to the season, but the cost to the planet of South African melons in November or Dutch tomatoes in January is enormous. Out of season produce is grown by fighting nature. Early tomatoes grow in hothouses, which need to be heated and lit consuming vast amounts of energy and chemicals. Produce grown further afield (although in season) is picked before it is ripe, treated with preservatives and then shipped across the globe. Delicate produce, such as strawberries or freshly cut flowers, is transported by plane, appearing on the shelves within 24 hours of being picked.

The major supermarket chains sell an identical range of fresh produce, paying little regard to the seasonal and regional variations available. Although Britain has around 6,000 native varieties of apple, only eight or nine are on sale in most shops, mostly from abroad. Native orchards are a haven for plants and wildlife as well as being an integral part of the landscape. Supermarkets insist on perfectly shaped unblemished produce, often to the detriment of flavour and smell. This makes it difficult for small farmers unable to meet the supermarkets' strict standards. The more perfect the fruit, the more it will have been sprayed with chemicals or wrapped in plastic whilst it was growing.

'Scrubbed and peated' potatoes are potatoes which have been washed and scrubbed and then sprinkled in peat, which brushes off easily, to make them look dirty and 'natural'.

The amount of artificial fertilisers, pesticides and other chemicals used on crops is causing increasing concern about damage to the environment and to human health from chemical residues left in food. Government research into residues in vegetables discovered 'unexpectedly high levels of acutely toxic pesticides' in carrots. Peeling removes 80% of pesticides, which still leaves residues of 20%. Based on the same research, Ethical Consumer magazine recommend avoiding non-organic carrots, potatoes and lettuces. Instead, they suggest eating asparagus, green cabbage, cauliflower, cucumber, garlic, leek, marrows, frozen peas (not tinned), pumpkins and squashes.

see Food page 110

Meat and Land Use

Increasing numbers of people are becoming vegetarian or cutting down on the amount of meat they eat. Apart from ethical concerns about cruelty to animals, there are compelling environmental and social reasons for reducing meat intake.

Millions of people throughout the world continually face starvation, caused by drought, soil erosion and economic pressures. Many more do not have adequate food or water. The drought in south-central Africa is affecting over ten countries, threatening some 20 million people. With increasing pressure on land from growing populations, along with worsening drought and desertification through climate change, we need to find ways of feeding the world's population.

In Thailand, between 1975 and 1985, many thousands of kilometres of forest were cleared to grow tapioca to export to the EEC as animal feed. It takes 16kg of feed to produce 1kg of beef.

If people ate less meat, more land would be available to grow crops for human consumption. More than 40% of the world's cereal production is used to feed livestock, occupying land that could be used to grow food for human consumption. Many poorer countries use valuable land to grow food to export as livestock feed to support western diets. In 1986, the year of Live Aid, a survey found that the Third World exported more food to the west than it imported, including food aid.

For every one calorie we get from beef, ten calories will have been consumed by the cow, an incredibly wasteful method of food production.

In the industrialised north we eat far more meat than people in other parts of the world. In the UK, we consume on average 75kg per person per year, compared with 1.1kg per person in India. There is great potential to reduce our meat intake, particularly given concerns over heart disease in Scotland.

Many animals destined for food are reared in appalling conditions. Chickens are not the only creatures in battery cages – pigs and many cattle suffer the same fate. They are routinely injected with growth hormones, antibiotics and other chemicals. These chemicals are absorbed into the human body, posing huge health risks and making diseases more resistant to antibiotics.

see Wholefoods page 45

Try to reduce your meat intake, and buy organic and free range meat whenever you can.

Supermarkets and Local Shops

Varieties of Scottish Apples:

Bloody Ploughman
Coul Blush
Early Julyan
Lady of the Wemyss
Stirling Castle
White Melrose
James Grieve
Galloway Pippin
Cambusnethan Pippin
Hawthornden
Lass O'Gowrie
Oslin (Arbroath Pippin)

Varieties of apple sold in average supermarket:

Golden Delicious (France)
Granny Smith's (South Africa)
Cox' Pippin (New Zealand)

Shopping habits have changed dramatically over the past 20 years. Small, specialised local shops have given way to ever larger supermarkets and out-of-town shopping centres. The trend towards supermarkets has had a range of knock-on effects, including a dramatic reduction in jobs. In 1989, one large supermarket chain owned 16% of the groceries market, employing 38,000 people full time. In 1950, the same 16% was owned by small independent shops employing 130,000 people full time. This trend is still increasing with more out-of-town shopping centres and hypermarkets being built across the country, whilst local shopping centres fall into decline.

Each supermarket chain has a complex delivery system designed to keep all branches fully stocked every hour of the day. Usually one or two huge warehouses supply the supermarket network by road. Every night, thousands of juggernauts travel thousands of miles to supply all of Britain's supermarkets, with more lorries still supplying the distribution centres themselves.

Shopping locally supports the local economy and cuts down on the need for transport – for customers and for the produce which is more likely to be locally-sourced than in supermarkets. Some items may be more expensive, but others will be cheaper. Fish from a fishmonger's, for instance, is cheaper and with less packaging than from a supermarket.

A Scottish-grown organic turnip was found on sale in an Edinburgh supermarket that had been packaged in Essex. Turnips do not need to be wrapped in plastic, much less driven 800 miles for the privilege. The benefits of buying a Scottish organic product were more than wiped out by the air pollution caused by packaging and transporting it.

Supermarkets do not offer the wide choice of products they claim to, compared to a good town or neighbourhood centre with high quality shops. The products in a supermarket pale next to the range available in fruit and vegetable shops, health and wholefood shops, butchers, fishmongers and bakeries. Support your local shops and your local economy as much as you can, and avoid driving to out-of-town supermarkets and shopping centres.

The Gyle shopping centre, on the edge of Edinburgh, attracts 80,000 cars a week and has been identified as the major source of traffic pollution in the west of the city. The irony is that the shopping centre recently won an award for the quality of its indoor air, which is ventilated and purified.

Fair Trade

Cash crops and other agricultural produce from developing countries are often produced under dangerous working conditions, using workers paid subsistence wages whilst multinational companies make huge profits at the expense of the environment.

Fair trade seeks to guarantee that those growing and picking crops are given the best terms possible for their produce. For small-holders producing crops such as cocoa and coffee, price fluctuations on the world market can undermine long term investment plans and consequently their security. When world prices fall below production costs, peoples jobs and livelihoods are at stake.

see Food page 110

Fair trade organisations pay a fair price direct to the producers, usually small, locally based co-operatives. They work closely with local producers and communities to make sure that workers are paid fair wages and have acceptable living conditions. A proportion of the profits is ploughed back into the community in the form of health care and schooling. There is also long term investment in sustainable agriculture which will meet the community's long term needs. Workers benefit from improved health and safety standards, and strict codes of practice mean that the local environment is damaged as little as possible.

By guaranteeing stable and competitive prices, farmers are less likely to be pressured by debt and poverty into growing cocaine and other drugs. These are often far more lucrative than staple crops whose prices can fluctuate widely on the world market.

In Britain, the Fairtrade Foundation was set up by, amongst others, Christian Aid and Oxfam to promote fair trade products here and in developing countries. In other European countries, fair trade schemes have been running for many years and both the Dutch and European Parliaments stock fair trade coffee as their 'official beverage'. In the UK, fair trade products are sold in health and whole-food shops and increasingly in supermarkets. Although the products may sometimes be more expensive, you can be sure that your money is not going to huge multinationals but is safeguarding both human rights and the environment. The best-known fair trade product is Cafedirect coffee.

Tea and Coffee

Tea and coffee are both cash crops produced in the Third World mainly for export. 48 million tonnes of coffee are produced every year in around 25 countries, mainly in Africa and Latin America. Tea is grown mainly in Asia, with India, China and Sri Lanka accounting for 57% of the world's trade. Britain is the second largest consumer of tea in the world after Ireland, and we still dominate the world trade in this crop.

Cafedirect Fair Trade coffee.

The wages and conditions of tea pickers are notoriously bad. Pickers are mostly poorly educated women and children whose wages range from 30p to £1 a day. Conditions are similar in the coffee industry. By buying fair trade tea and coffee, you are directly improving the conditions of the workers on the plantations. Tea and especially coffee have a heavy toll on the environment. Both are intensively grown cash crops taking up huge tracts of land and requiring vast inputs of chemicals. Coffee quickly exhausts the soil, needing even more fertilisers and chemicals.

see Tea page 111

Tea – Although convenient, try to avoid tea bags. They cost up to 20% more than loose tea and contain more tea leaves than needed. Don't buy overpackaged tea in individually wrapped tea bags or foil-wrapped sachets. Organic tea is available. Fair trade teas can be bought in bulk, saving money and packaging.

It takes 18000 calories of energy to make a kilo of instant coffee.

Coffee – Fresh coffee is better for the environment than instant, with less energy and packaging used in production. Instant coffee costs less but doesn't taste as good. Fair trade coffee is widely available.

Herbal Teas – Herbal and fruit teas don't have the environmental impact of black teas and are becoming more popular. Organic and loose-leaf herbal teas are available, but they are often in individually wrapped sachets. Herbs such as mint grow easily in a pot – two leaves in a cup of boiling water and you have a cheap and green cup of herbal tea.

Water: Bottled or Tap?

We are buying ever increasing quantities of bottled water in a whole variety of shapes, flavours and fizziness. There are two types of bottled water – spring water and mineral water. Spring water is merely water from a natural spring. Mineral water must be bottled at source and usually contains varying amounts of minerals with various health benefits. For a balanced chemical intake, you should vary what you drink.

Does water really need to be packaged?

Bottled Water – This has a huge environmental impact. It has to be bottled, packaged and then transported, consuming energy and resources before drunk. The bottles are then thrown away, at a rate of over 700,000 million per year. Bottled water is rarely sold in recyclable glass bottles. Most is sold packaged in plastic. There is none available in returnable deposit bottles.

Tap Water – Tap water is free and does not need to be packed or transported long distance. Although it requires some treatment, it is still better than bottled water. Scottish tap water is sourced from lochs and reservoirs rather than from rivers and is usually of a very high quality and considerably purer than in other parts of the UK.

see Local Authorities page 122

The EU imposes strict targets for water quality, and domestic supplies are regularly scrutinised. All householders have the right to have their supply checked for quality and pollutants by their local authority, and to have problems remedied. If you have concerns about the purity of your water supply contact your local authority.

Wholefoods

Wholefoods are simply staple foods which have not been cooked, prepared or processed. Wholefoods include rice and other grains, nuts and pulses as well as fruit, vegetables and cuts of meat.

Wholefoods are generally cheaper than processed food and with more guarantee of quality ingredients. Unprocessed with less packaging, they save energy and money. Although many supermarkets now sell wholefoods, they invariably charge more and over-package. Health and wholefood shops generally stock a much wider range of products.

Soya beans, chick peas, lentils, rice and grains, nuts and pulses are all integral to daily diets around the world. They are versatile, easy to prepare and filling, as well as cheaper than processed equivalents. Vegetarian cookery books contain recipes for most wholefoods. Cookery books specialising in foreign cookery are even better. Soya beans (rich in protein), cooked with garlic and herbs, tomatoes and other vegetables are a common feature in Mediterranean meals.

303kg of synthetic fertiliser are put on each hectare of UK farmland.

As well as being cheaper, a diet based on wholefoods and other natural ingredients, avoids artificial additives and other harmful ingredients. The additives and 'E' numbers found to be harmful ten years ago are still put in our foods but under different names. E211, a preservative found in many fizzy drinks and linked to asthma, is now more commonly found on the ingredients list under its real name sodium benzoate. Some additives are perfectly safe. Some cause rare but extreme allergies. Others are generally associated with hyperactivity, irritability and other behavioural problems, particularly in children.

At least 500 species of insect, including major pests, are known to have become resistant to chemical pesticides.

With additives including 'natural' ones such as salt and sugar, present in so many foods, the only guaranteed way of avoiding them is to cook using whole ingredients.

A Green Shopping List

Glass milk bottles can be used up to 40 times

Milk – Milk is a staple item in most households. Until fairly recently milk delivery was a perfect example of a locally-based distribution system. Most milk was produced and drunk locally. It was delivered in glass bottles, which on average were used 40 times. Cheap packaging, supermarkets and changing legislation have almost killed off doorstep milk deliveries, but they are still available in many areas. You will find details in the Yellow Pages. Environmental audits show that the best option after glass bottles is to buy one or two pints in cartons and larger amounts in plastic bottles.

Salt – Rock salt should be avoided. It has to be mined, causing similar environmental problems to other types of mining. Sea salt, however, requires less energy as most of it is produced by evaporating sea water in shallow basins using solar energy. Buying salt in large packets is cheaper and saves packaging.

Tinned, Bottled, Frozen or Irradiated – Each of these is a method of preserving food longer than it otherwise would, and each has its environmental advantages and disadvantages. Look for products with the least packaging. Tins consume energy and resources during manufacture, but can be recycled. Glass can also be recycled, whereas plastic rarely can. Frozen food consumes energy throughout its life, but a large bag of frozen peas saves packaging in the long run, especially in an efficiently-running freezer.

Irradiated food has been blasted with radiation to kill bacteria and to preserve it longer, in transit, in the shop and in your home. Irradiation depends upon radio-active elements sourced from the highly-polluting nuclear industry. Avoid irradiated food – there is no need for it and the long term health effects are unknown. Irradiated food should be clearly labelled as such.

see Food page 110 for Fairtrade sugar

Sugar – Buy sugar made from European sugar beet, preferably grown in the UK, rather than from sugar cane which will have been produced in the Caribbean and transported long distance. Although we need a certain amount of sugar, many of us eat far too much, especially as it is already added to many processed foods. Reduce your sugar intake and look for foods with no added sugar.

16% of the energy needed to produce a loaf of white bread is for packaging and transport.

Flour and Bread – It is best to buy wholemeal or wholewheat flour as it contains the whole of the wheat grain with nothing added or taken away. Brown flour contains only around 85% of the original wheat, and white flour 75% or less. Wholemeal flour contains all the original vitamins and minerals, whereas many of these are lost in processing brown and white flour, and then have to be added to bring them up to at least 80% of the original. Wholemeal flour is more nutritious with more fibre than other flours, needing less energy and artificial ingredients to produce. Organic wholemeal flour and bread is becoming more widely available, especially from health and wholefood shops. Organic bread contains no preservatives, so goes stale quicker. Keep it in the fridge to make it last longer.

Fruit Juice – Most of the orange juice drunk in Britain comes from Brazil. The production of one tonne of Brazilian orange juice consumes at least 25 tonnes of materials, including 22 tonnes of water and 0.1 tonne of fuel, making it a very costly drink in environmental terms. Oranges and other citrus fruits need plenty of irrigation and chemical sprays. They then need to be transported long distance to reach Britain. Apple and blackcurrant juice are locally-grown alternatives, need little in the way of irrigation or pesticides, are much more resource efficient and contain as many vitamins as orange juice.

Chocolate – As with tea, coffee and other cash crops in developing countries, land and vegetation is often cleared to make way for cocoa plantations. Underpaid plantation workers work under dangerous conditions, often in contact with pesticides banned or restricted in many other countries. Traces of these pesticides are often found in the chocolate we eat. In 1992, in Britain, we spent £2.9 billion on chocolate, which represents many thousands of acres of cocoa plantation. The relatively cheap price of a chocolate bar in Britain hides the enormous amount of energy needed to produce it and transport it thousands of miles. By law, a chocolate bar need only contain as little as 20% cocoa solids, with the rest made up of sugar and cheap oils. You can buy organic fair trade chocolateor just cut down how much you eat. Don't buy hideously over-packaged chocolate.

see Food page 110

The Kitchen

The Greener Cleaning Cupboard

Green cleaning shopping list:

Soda crystals
Table salt
White distilled vinegar
Bicarbonate of soda
Nylon scourers
Washable dishcloth
Lemon juice
Borax
String mop
Brush with replaceable head

Looking at the supermarket shelves, it would seem that you need a separate detergent for cleaning each different part of the house – for the windows, for the floor, for the toilet, for kitchen tiles, for dusting and even for cleaning skirting boards and other wooden surfaces. The fact is, the bulk of these products contain practically identical ingredients and in many cases are just pre-diluted versions of cleaners you could make yourself.

Although pressure from consumers has forced some detergent manufacturers to make some changes towards more environmentally-friendly products, many cleaning products still pose a variety of problems to the environment and to the user. The lack of laws on green labelling in the UK allows companies to invent their own labels for their products, which mean nothing and confuse the consumer. The EU Eco-Label now applies to some detergents.

Several companies specialise in environmentally-friendly cleaning products, made from renewable vegetable-based ingredients, which biodegrade faster than oil-based ones. The ingredients aren't tested on animals. Some companies sell their products in refillable packaging, at a price discount and most healthfood shops will sell eco-friendly detergents, if your usual shops don't.

Whichever products you buy, make sure you only use as much as you need, bearing in mind that Scotland has very soft water so smaller quantities of detergent go much further than in hard water areas. For dishwashers and washing machines, use powder rather than liquid.

Cloths, Scourers, Mops....

Dishcloths – Most households use lots of these, often buying the cheap disposable kind in packs of ten or twenty. For the same price you can buy two or three cotton dishcloths which you can wash with your laundry. White cloths inevitably go brown after a while, but don't soak them in bleach. A stained cloth will normally still be clean, but if you prefer, whiten it by soaking it overnight in soda crystals. When the cloth has finished its useful life in the kitchen, use it elsewhere, e.g. for cleaning the toilet or your bicycle.

Scourer Pads – Sponges with green scourer pads attached don't last long. Nylon and wire wool scourers last much longer. A home-made option is to save the plastic netting onions come in and use that instead.

Mops – A proper string mop lasts longer than cheaper foam versions. You can buy replacement heads for some mops, but the heads can be washed in the washing machine (wrap a tea towel around the plastic bit) or soaked overnight in soda crystals. A common practice abroad is to tie a floor cloth to a brush and then wash the cloth afterwards.

see Washing-Up
page 115

Washing Up and Scrubbing Brushes – Wooden-handled brushes, with natural fibre bristles, are much better for the environment than plastic and nylon ones. They last a lot longer and can be made from renewable resources. Brushes sold by Friends of the Earth have handles made from sustainably-produced beech and bristles from the fibres of unbleached tropical plants. You can also get brushes with replaceable heads. These are more expensive initially but cheaper in the long run. Use a wooden brush for scrubbing vegetables, except for non-organic ones which you should always peel. Buy brooms and other floor brushes made from wood and natural bristles.

Whenever you can, try to re-use things you already have around the home instead of buying things especially, like dusters which can be made from old T-shirts. Downgrade older items to the bathroom or the garage. Toothbrushes have a long life ahead of them once they are too worn to brush your teeth with.

Alternative Cleaning Products

Soda crystals cost less than £1 a kilo. They are usually available in hardware shops and sometimes chemists. Some supermarkets still sell them.

Soda crystals – Sodium carbonate crystals, also known as washing soda, used to be the most common household cleaning product and, used sparingly, are much better for the environment than most other detergents. Amongst other uses, they act as a water softener which, when added to washing powder, mean you can use less normal detergent. To use, dissolve the crystals in warm water, using different amounts for weaker or stronger solutions, depending on what you need to clean. A solution of soda crystals is odourless and, because it doesn't froth up, it is easier to rinse off than other detergents. Another feature of soda crystals is that they leave whatever they clean very shiny, making them ideal for tiles, cutlery and floors.

In the kitchen, use soda crystals for the floor, work surfaces and wall tiles, to soak the sink overnight to get rid of tea stains and to clean the draining board and taps with. Wherever there is grease, use a really strong mixture and add some salt to your cloth, or use a scourer pad if you need a stronger abrasive. You can add the crystals to your washing-up water and to your dishwasher powder for more effective cleaning, for shinier crockery and to use less washing up liquid and powder. Soaking greasy grill pans, barbecue grills and other kitchen implements in a hot strong mixture dissolves the dirt. Soda crystals are particularly recommended for cleaning the insides of fridges and freezers, as well as for cleaning plastic food containers and lunch boxes. You can soak dirty clothes in a soda crystal mixture before putting them in the washing machine, to get rid of stubborn stains.

The best way of cleaning the bottom of a dustbin is to soak it over night in a soda crystal solution. Don't use bleach.

Elsewhere in the house, use a weaker mixture of soda crystals for cork tiles, wooden floors and finger prints on doors and paintwork. Most of the bathroom can be cleaned using soda crystals.

Vinegar – White distilled vinegar, acetic acid, is very cheap. It is a good alternative to many other cleaning products, saving packaging, resources and the environment. Because it is a simple chemical, it is more easily broken down than stronger acids and cleaning agents and causes less harm to the environment.

Fill an empty pump action or plant spray with a half vinegar, half water solution to clean windows, tiles and mirrors. This can also be used for dusting and removing smudge and finger marks from polished wood, but wipe it off straight away. Rings and other stains on wood can be removed by polishing with a mixture of olive oil and vinegar.

A stronger solution of water and vinegar in a squeezy bottle cleans the toilet, but you may have to scrub it a bit with the toilet brush. Use the vinegar mixture for getting rid of scale on sinks and draining boards, in kettles, irons and coffee makers instead of shop-bought de-scalers

Lemon juice – Big bottles of lemon juice are relatively cheap and can be used for cleaning as well as cooking. Although lemon juice is an acid, it is a natural chemical and more easily broken down in the environment. You can use it instead of bleach to disinfect surfaces and the toilet. You can use it neat on a cloth for cleaning in between tiles, around the edges of baths and showers and for getting rid of the black bits at the base of taps.

Use lemon juice to polish silver. Soak tarnished silver in warm water and lemon juice and add a piece of silver foil wrapping or milk bottle top. Unless the silver is very badly tarnished or damaged, it comes out as good as new. The silver tarnish is removed by a process of electrolysis. Salt does the same.

Alternative Cleaning Products

Some brands of detergent are made from vegetable-based ingredients and come in refillable bottles.

Washing-up – Many famous brand named washing-up liquids come highly concentrated, but most people still use far more than is needed. Psychologically, the more bubbles in the sink, the better, but bubbles do nothing to make the dishes cleaner and some eco washing-up liquids don't froth at all. Use as little liquid as possible and don't be tempted to squirt in more as soon as the bubbles have disappeared. Add a tablespoon of soda crystals for added effect. To clean burnt saucepans and frying pans, instead of using diluted bleach, boil salty water until the burnt bits begin to come off.

Washing-up liquid and water is all you need for outside windows: dry the windows with newspapers, which guarantees a smear-free finish.

Polishing and dusting – Polishing wooden furniture with spray polish, either from an aerosol or a pump action spray, gives an instant shine to the surface but in the long run leaves a white smear. Proper wood surfaces should be polished with beeswax or another hard furniture polish and dusted only with a soft cloth; a water and vinegar solution gets rid of smudges and smears, as well as the smears left by aerosol spray polish.

Bicarbonate of Soda – Most commonly known as a raising agent for cooking, bicarbonate of soda is also an effective cleaning product around the house. It used to be used as a toothpaste: a wet toothbrush was dipped into the powder, making a paste. This has suddenly been rediscovered by big toothpaste companies, many of whom are busy bringing out bicarbonate of soda toothpastes.

Household Pests

Humane mousetraps catch mice without killing them. You then release them outside, although this may just mean the mouse ends up in someone else's home. Use a normal trap, which kills the mouse instantly, instead of using poison.

Most insect killers contain deadly chemicals, hence the warnings on the packets to keep the contents away from children and pets. Aerosol cans, apart from the excess packaging that they use, spray the poison around the room, contaminating everything. Other products are designed to be left lying around. Either way, deliberately bringing poisons into your home should be kept as a last resort, especially when alternatives exist.

Plants and less harmful products can be used to kill insects and other pests, but first try and find the source of the infestation. Set traps for crawling insects like cockroaches by putting sweets or sugar at the bottom of a jar with a ramp for them to get in but not to get out. For wasps, mix sugar or jam with water in a jar covered with clingfilm with a hole. The wasps can get in, but can't get out.

see Pest Control page 112

Flies – Fruit flies and other small flies can live in fruit bowls, the soil of pot plants, and damp wood or plaster. Try and eradicate them at source before resorting to more drastic measures. Flies hate basil and mint plants, so grow them inside in pots and outside near windows and doors. They also hate orange peel, lemon peel and cloves, which you can position strategically if you have a particular fly problem where you live. Better than spraying fly spray around your home is to use fly paper, which you can make yourself from brown paper and treacle. Fly swatters only harm insects and are environmentally safe.

Ants – Ants come in from outside, so first try to find their nest and pour a few kettle-fulls of boiling water down the holes. If you can't find the nest, sprinkle dried mint or chilli powder on the ground where they come in. Like flies, ants don't like mint, so plant it in your garden to keep them at bay.

Moths – Instead of using mothballs, which contain the toxic irritant pesticide paradichlorobenzene, hang lavender and cedar wood in amongst your clothes. If you have a moth problem, make sure you wash your clothes on a hot wash before hanging them in the wardrobe. This kills the moth eggs before they hatch.

Fridges and Freezers

If 80% of British fridge freezers were fitted with a saver plug, the electricity saving would be half the output of a nuclear power station.

You can increase the energy efficiency of your fridge and freezer by making sure that the thermostat is not set too high. Experiment to find the optimum temperature level and change the setting as the seasons change. The energy used to cool the air is far more than is needed simply to maintain it at the right temperature, so it is vital to keep fridges and freezers working as efficiently as possible.

Keep the Door Shut – Every time you open the door of the fridge/ freezer, cold air escapes and warm air replaces it. For every minute the door is open it takes many more for the inside temperature to get back down to the right level.

Keep the Cold Air In – To stop the cold air escaping, put small items in plastic containers at the front of the shelves to act as walls. Put empty boxes on empty shelves. If you have a small freezer compartment inside the fridge, make sure it shuts and seals properly. Chest freezers and freezers with drawers are best for keeping cold air in. If you have neither, keep food and containers near the front of the shelves. Keep the magnetic seals clean and make sure they grip tightly – a coating of Vaseline will help the door seal even tighter. Never put hot food in the fridge – wait until it has cooled down first.

Keep the Fridge Cool on the Outside – The warmer it is outside the fridge or the freezer, the more energy is needed to cool the inside. Because they produce heat, it is important to make sure that air can circulate around them. Don't put keep them too close to the wall or in a confined space. Put them far from radiators, ovens, washing machines and other sources of heat.

Many fridges get thrown away simply because the light bulb has broken! When yours goes, make sure you replace it. You may have to order it from the manufacturer.

Switch Off – If you have a garage, a conservatory or even a north-facing window ledge, you could switch off your fridge during the coldest winter months and keep essentials, such as milk, margarine or yoghurts, outside. If you do this you will need to buy provisions on a daily basis. Before going away on holiday, make sure you empty the fridge and switch it off. If you have a fridge freezer with only one control switch, turn the fridge thermostat down to the minimum setting. Better still, eat the food in the freezer or ask a friend to store it while you are away and switch it off completely.

see Savaplugs page 113

Fit a Savaplug – A fridge or freezer needs different amounts of energy at different stages in the cooling cycle. A Savaplug saves energy by matching the energy the fridge consumes with the amount it actually needs. Savaplugs cost around £20 and are best suited to older fridges. You can buy them from most DIY shops.

Don't be tempted to buy over-packaged convenience food to fill the freezer. You can freeze all sorts of food including bread, soft fruit, home-made soups and other meals. Cooking extra to freeze and eat later saves money, resources and time.

Buying a New Fridge or Freezer

Keeping Your Old One – Does your old fridge or freezer really need to be replaced? Could it be repaired and thoroughly cleaned? An electrician can mend most faults, a glass cutter can replace broken shelves and you can order spare parts from the manufacturer. Getting hold of spares may sometimes be difficult, as products often seem to be designed to be thrown away, rather than repaired. However they are likely to be available somewhere, so persevere. Fitting a Savaplug will make your old machine more energy-efficient.

see Savaplugs page 113

Buying Second Hand – This may save money and resources but second hand models will not display energy labels (see below), so you will not be able to compare the energy efficiency of different makes. Second hand models will invariably consume more energy than new models, so look for the smallest and newest appliance you can find, preferably without a freezer compartment (always the first part to go wrong) and fit a Savaplug. All second hand fridges and freezers will contain CFCs and require careful disposal. Buying a second-hand fridge or freezer is fraught with problems – in this case it is probably best to buy new.

see Local Authorities · page 122

Disposing of Your Old Fridge – Fridges and freezers are not like other types of household waste because of their CFC content. If the appliance is still in working order you could take it to a second-hand dealer, who will either pay for it or simply take it off your hands. Failing that, contact your local authority Environmental Services Department to ask for a special collection and CFC recycling. Fridges and freezers should never ever be dumped.

Greener fridges and freezers are increasingly available. These are more energy efficient and use coolants which do not damage the ozone layer or contribute to climate change. If you intend to buy new you can invest in a model with real long term environmental and cost savings. Any extra money spent on a green make will save money in the long term. Fridges are covered by the EU Eco-Label.

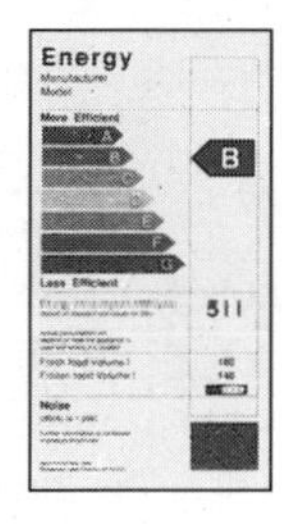

Energy Efficiency – All new fridges and freezers must display an EU energy label showing energy consumption. Try to choose the most energy efficient appliance, but also only buy one the right size for your needs. If you already have a freezer, don't buy a new fridge with a freezer compartment.

Chest freezers are the best type of freezer to buy as the cold air does not escape when the door is opened. An upright freezer with interior doors goes some way to preventing air fall-out, especially when divided into two sections with a main door for each.

see Ozone Layer page 35

HFC gases are 3,200 times more powerful than carbon dioxide. By 2005, world-wide emissions of HFCs are estimated to be over 230,000 tonnes, the equivalent of the UK's CO_2 output.

contact Greenpeace for details of green fridges, see page 121

Manufacturer's Guarantee – The longer the product lasts the better. The guarantee indicates how long the manufacturer thinks the product will last. Compare the different guarantees and choose the best.

Don't buy CFCs, HFCs and HCFCs – Even fridges and freezers which don't contain CFCs may still contain the other ozone-damaging chemicals HCFCs or the greenhouse gases HFCs, which are also used as refrigerants. HFCs are often used instead of CFCs but are powerful greenhouse gases. Appliances based on naturally-occurring substances, such as hydrocarbons, ammonia and carbon dioxide are available, but need careful disposal.

Washing Machine, Tumble Dryer, Dishwasher

Washing Machines – Don't run a wash for small loads unless you have an economy or half load setting, remembering to adjust the amount of powder you use accordingly. Washing on lower temperatures also uses less energy, but there are increasing concerns that these lower temperatures contribute to the increase in asthma as the water is not hot enough to kill dust mites found in fabrics. Look for environmentally-friendly detergents, either a well-known brand or bearing the EU Eco-Label.

Launderettes – These are the greenest option. Shared machines save on resources and the washing machines are far more energy-efficient than dometic machines as the water is centrally heated, usually by gas. Launderettes have a range of different-sized machines, letting you choose the right size for the amount of washing you have, and if drying your clothes at home is a problem, the gas-powered tumble dryers are far more efficient than electric ones.

see Clothes Airers page 110

Clothes Drying – Why use a tumble dryer? Drying your clothes naturally, either outside or in, uses no resources whatsoever and costs you nothing. Most tenement flats have access to a back green for drying clothes, and if there are no washing poles, contact your local authority or speak to your neighbours about getting some. Failing that, a clothes horse can easily be put outside. Many flats are installing a line-and-pulley system on a simple wooden frame from a back window. Some of these are home-made. High-ceilinged flats are ideal for clothes pulleys, which are rapidly coming back into fashion. Cheaper and more convenient still is a pullout clothes line, usually fitted above a bath.

An electric tumble dryer is very energy intensive, especially for drying heavy items like jeans, bedclothes and towels. If you have one, use it only when you really have to. A major problem with tumble dryers is the outflow pipe, taking out the hot air. Because of the dust the pipe should go directly outside, but think of the waste as you pump hot air straight outside.

Buying A New Machine

Some washing machines, dishwashers, and tumble dryers, are or will soon carry Eco-Labels. Contact Friends of the Earth Scotland to find out which makes have qualified.

Before throwing any machine away, see whether it can be repaired or taken to a second hand shop. Is it still under guarantee? If so, what are the conditions? Can the machine be part-exchanged, meaning it may be disassembled and recycled?

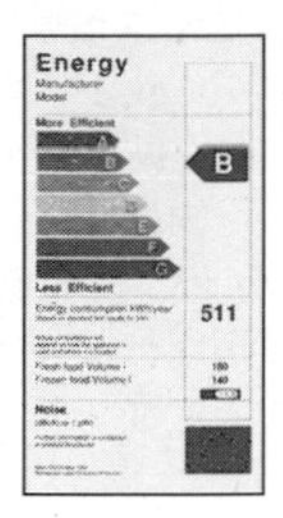

Energy Efficiency – Look for the EU energy label. The most efficient washing machines are able to take in water direct from your hot water system. This is normally far more efficient than heating the water inside the machine, particularly if you have a gas heating system. Some washing machines and tumble dryers weigh the washing, adapting washing and drying times and the amount of hot water needed accordingly. Moisture detectors in tumble dryers switch the machine off when the washing is dry. Buy a machine with an economy load option.

Water and Detergent Consumption – For dishwashers and washing machines, check water consumption (one criteria of the Eco-Label), and whether they have any other 'eco-features' such as detergent recycling systems. Machines which automatically weigh the washing load can alter how much energy, water and detergent they use.

see Buying a New Fridge page 56

Ask about the reparability of each model. Check the manufacturer's guarantee to see which make is likely to last longer and which has the best conditions for repairs and servicing.

Appliances

Carving knives, can openers, toothbrushes, blenders, coffee grinders, coffee machines, toasters, cork screws, potato peelers, orange squeezers, knife sharpeners, table Hoovers, cappuccino/expresso machines, pasta makers, yoghurt makers, ice cream makers, sandwich toasters, chip pans, slow cookers, teas-made, cheese-graters, egg-poachers, mixers and whisks: all of them are electric machines for doing household tasks that can easily be done by hand or using something else.

Individually, each gadget consumes hardly any energy and whilst cutting down on their use may not seem a high environmental priority, the combined effects of many thousands of gadgets in millions of homes all add up. A green home would have and would use as few electric gadgets as possible. As well as energy consumption, gadgets use packaging and are made of a myriad different types of plastic, metals and heavy metals and are impossible to recycle or repair, even when the facilities exist.

As for everything that you buy, choose products that are durable, reparable and that you really need. Don't buy items that will go out of fashion or will loose their novelty within weeks or months. Soda streams, which were a huge success in the 1970s, became totally useless once the gas cylinder refills became hard to find in the shops when the fad had passed.

Toaster – A toaster is far more efficient for making toast than under the grill where a lot of the heat is lost. A toaster concentrates the heat only where it is needed and because the bread is closer to the heat than under a grill, it toasts faster. The drawback is when one slice of bread is toasted in a toaster designed for four. Buy one well-suited to your needs in terms of size.

Food blender – To make your own food from your own ingredients, a food blender is a vital piece of equipment. The energy and money you save by doing this more than outweighs the small amount consumed by the blender.

Kettle – Flimsy plastic kettles don't last very long, they break easily and are almost impossible to repair. Boiling water in an electric kettle uses a lot less energy than in a pan or even in a stove-top kettle, especially on an electric cooker. Only ever boil as much water as you need. If your kettle doesn't have a level indicator on the side, open the lid to fill it, instead of pouring the water through the spout. This lets you see how far you've filled it. When you need boiling water for cooking, boil it first in the kettle instead of in the saucepan.

Steel kettles last the longest and although they cost more to buy, they save you money in the long run. If you have to buy a new one, make sure it has a level indicator. If you have a gas stove, you can buy kettles with special fittings around the base that keep in the heat, concentrating it on the underneath rather than losing it into the room.

Dishwashers – Only run a wash when the machine is full, but don't use extra crockery and cutlery just because you don't have to wash them up yourself. Wash up by hand after small meals or when part of the family is away, rather than leaving the dirt to dry onto the dishes in the machine. To save energy during the programme, switch the dishwasher off before the drying stage and open the door: the plates will still be hot enough to dry on their own. Look for environmentally-friendly detergents, either a well-known brand or bearing the EU Eco-Label. Use powder instead of liquid.

Energy-Efficient Cooking

Cooking with gas is 40% more efficient than with electricity.

Saucepans – Cooking with a lid uses four times less energy than cooking without. Leaving the lid off lets the steam and the heat out, needing more energy to keep the food at the same temperature. If you keep the lid on, you can boil a pan of water at a lower setting and cut down on steam in the kitchen. Cook two items at once by putting a colander on top. Then put the lid on. Pan dividers allow you to boil several different vegetables at once.

Flat bottomed pans are better than domed ones as they make contact with the whole ring. Use the right sized ring for the pan you are using and always use the smallest pan and ring you can. Use as little water as possible and boil it first in the kettle instead of in the pan. Electric rings take a while to cool down, so turn them off a few minutes before the food is cooked. Don't buy aluminium saucepans. If you already have these, don't cook acidic food, such as rhubarb or soft fruit, in them as the acid strips the aluminium which leaches into your food.

Cooking in the Oven – It takes a lot of energy to heat up an oven, so try to cook more than one dish at a time to get maximum use of the heat. Secondary glass doors on ovens keep the heat in when the main door is open. Try to keep this clean so you can see how your cooking is progressing without losing all the heat. Don't leave the oven door open, and switch off a few minutes before you take the food out.

Microwave cooking – If you already have a microwave oven, careful and efficient use (i.e. *not* defrosting whole chickens) can result in some energy savings. A new microwave oven costs energy and resources to make and any energy savings will take a long time to pay back. On the whole, use your microwave sparingly. Energy-efficient cooking on a gas stove is a much better option.

Barbecue Charcoal – If you have a barbecue, choose a locally-grown source of charcoal. One DIY chain sells charcoal produced locally to each branch.

Extractor Fans – If you have an extractor fan in your kitchen, use it as little as possible - keeping the lid on boiling pans of water for instance, keeps steam to a minimum. Open the window instead of switching on the fan. Instead of installing a new electric fan, look for a plastic fan which fits into your window and works by using differences in air pressure between the inside of the kitchen and outside.

Coffee Machines – A coffee filter machine simply dribbles hot water through the coffee powder. This uses a lot of energy and plastic for something you could easily do by hand with a kettle and a plastic filter over a jug. Filter machines use an electric hot plate to keep the coffee warm, although some machines do have lower heat settings for when the coffee jug is half full. Instead, use a jug thermos flask to serve the coffee which keeps the coffee warm using no energy. Rather than disposable paper coffee filters, buy a plastic or cotton re-usable filter. They are easily rinsed and the cotton filter can be put in the washing machine every so often.

A coffee percolator uses less energy and resources than an electric coffee filter.

Better than a filter machine is a cafetiere with a plunger. Made with only a few parts and costing less, the only energy required is to heat the kettle, which is far more efficient, provided you only boil the amount of water you actually need. The next best option is a stove-top coffee percolator, particularly if you have a gas cooker. If you cook with electricity, fill it with boiling water from the kettle first. For gas or electricity, make sure you use the appropriate size of ring.

Recycling in your Kitchen
Composting Kitchen Waste

If you have access to a garden, composting kitchen (and garden) waste makes substantial environmental savings and is one of the most ecologically-sound things you can do in your home. Composting completes the natural cycle of returning organic materials back to the soil and is the ultimate in home recycling. The compost you make can then be used in your own garden and is the greenest alternative to peat, which is extracted widely in the Highlands and Ireland, destroying fragile ecosystems. Even the smallest garden should have room for a compost bin or heap, and if you live in a tenement building with a common stair and a back green, then think about setting up a communal composting system.

see Waste Disposal page 28

Some 35 million tonnes of kitchen and garden waste end up being dumped in landfill sites across the UK. As it rots, it produces an explosive greenhouse gas, methane, and liquid seeps into the water table surrounding the landfill site, causing water pollution. Apart from turning an otherwise waste product back into soil, if compostable materials (i.e. 'wet waste') were removed from household waste, it would be much easier for local authorities to sort everything else (plastic, metal, paper...) for recycling.

Elsewhere in Europe composting is common. In the Netherlands door to door collections of compostable waste is compulsory. In Denmark, more than 10% of households have doorstep compost collections.

Composting is the natural process of breaking down organic waste into soil by the bacteria, worms and insects present in the compost heap. All you have to do is add your kitchen and garden waste to your heap, water occasionally and spread the contents on your garden when it is ready. Although composting is a straightforward operation, its success and the soil you end up with depend on what you put in.

Where to Compost – You can either build your own compost bin in a corner of the garden, use an old plastic barrel or dustbin or buy a specially made compost bin, often made out of recycled plastic. Using a compost bin takes up a lot less space outside than does making your own heap, but make sure it hasn't got a bottom and sits on bare soil to allow for drainage and for the worms and other creatures to get in. A lid is important, to keep the heat in and cats and foxes out. In summer, a lid stops any smells from escaping.

What to Compost – It is important to have the right mixture of material going into your bin: too many dry, woody ingredients and the composting won't happen, too much wet and green stuff and the compost will end up slimy and smelly. The more stuff you put in your compost bin at once, the hotter it will get and the faster it will decompose, especially at the start. All the vegetable matter from your kitchen can go into the compost bin, but meat and fish may attract cats, foxes and occasionally rats unless the heap is well sealed.

How to Store it in the Kitchen – It is very unlikely that the compost will start to smell in your kitchen unless you keep it for ages or if it is in a sealed container. If you produce lots of compostable material then keep a small bin or bucket in your kitchen and empty it every so often. If you don't produce very much, then keep an old margarine or ice cream tub somewhere convenient for tea bags and other small bits of waste. Try not to use plastic carrier bags.

30% of household waste is compostable

The Rest of your Kitchen Waste – When you have started composting and recycling everything else, all you should be throwing away is non-recyclable plastic and other odd items. Only put your rubbish out when the bag is really full and cut down on the amount of bin bags you use. If you are composting properly then the bin won't smell, especially if you rinse milk cartons before binning them. If your council doesn't give you free bin bags, try and buy recycled ones.

Recycling in your Kitchen

Recycling what you would otherwise throw away is not as simple as just throwing it in the bin, it needs a bit of forethought and planning. Find your nearest recycling banks.If they are not within walking or cycling distance, then only drive there when you are on the way somewhere else: don't take the car especially (unless you have got a whole year's supply). Contact your council's Environmental Health Department for details of recycling banks in your area and if there are none near you, write to the council and ask why.

see Local Authorities page 122

Washing your Recyclables – Tin cans and bottles should be washed, which also stops them from smelling if you have to store them for a while before taking them to the recycling banks. Cans should also have their labels peeled off before being recycled. When you open a can of food, don't cut the lid right off: leave it hanging on and push it inside when the can is empty to avoid cutting yourself. Wash what your recyclables with the washing up, and squash cans so they take up less space. Can crushers are available.

see Can Crushers page 109

Storing your Recyclables – Establish a convenient way of storing your recyclables. The more you get through, the more space you will need; another incentive to cut down on the amount of packaging you buy. Keeping everything in cloth bags seems to be the best way. Hang the bags in the kitchen and just take them with you when you go to the recycling banks, washing the bags every so often with your normal laundry. Paper, especially newspaper, is particularly bulky so find a big and tough bag, cloth or otherwise, for it.

Kitchen Appliances – In some areas electric appliances, such as toasters and kettles, can be recycled. Contact your council, the Recycling Advisory Group for Scotland or Friends of the Earth for local details.

see Recycling page 112

Plastic – Some local authorities offer domestic plastic recycling facilities. The number should increase in the future.

see Local Authorities page 122

Junk Mail – Paper can be recycled, but better still contact the Mailing Preference Service to have your name taken off all mailing lists.

see Mailing Preference Service page 127

Energy for Heating and Hot Water

Immersion Heater – Electric immersion heaters heat the water in a boiler. Homes with gas powered heating and hot water systems may still have an immersion heater, but try to use it only in an emergency as although it heats the water faster, electricity is less efficient than gas. Storing hot water in a boiler inevitably wastes energy through gradual heat loss. Make sure the hot water tank and pipes are properly insulated. If your tank has a thermostatic control set it at low. If the water is scalding hot, too much energy is being used. Keep the thermostat on the tank firmly fixed to the side and make sure it is not covered by insulation.

Timer Switches – Electric immersion heaters tend not to have timers, but they should never be left on all the. It normally takes an hour to heat up a tank of water, and a properly lagged tank should stay hot overnight, so for hot water first thing in the morning it should be enough to switch on for an hour before going to bed, rather than leaving it on all night. Off-peak or white meter electricity is cheaper, but you should still use as little as possible.

You can get timer switches in electrical or DIY shops for £19-£30. Install a thermostat in your tank if you do not already have one.

Lagging the Hot Water Tank – Properly lagging the hot water tank reduces heat loss by 75%. If your hot tank is in the loft, it is especially important to keep it well insulated. Check to see whether your tank is already lagged – if you live in a modern house, or have a relatively recent hot water system, then it probably is. Some tanks have a mustard yellow fitted spray-foam lining, others have a tied-on jacket. The spray foam lining is generally very efficient, but if it is less than two inches thick, cover it with an additional tie-on one. Any new insulating jacket should bear the British Standard number BS5615:1985 and will cost around £5-£10.

see Energy Advice Centres page 119

Instant Hot Water Systems – Instant hot water systems, such as condensing gas boilers, heat water on demand and, depending on the system, supply water to both the taps and the heating. Condensing boilers recover a large proportion of the heat from the burnt flue gases and, as such, they are highly efficient. Although these types of boiler cost more to install, they achieve efficiencies of over 90% and will save money and energy after only a short period, depending on how much you use.

The Bathroom

The average person in Scotland uses 325 litres of water every day. 90% of the UK's fresh water is in Scotland, and although Scotland has plentiful supplies (unlike many parts of England), we should still try to use less than we do. All domestic water supply, whether for drinking or for washing, has to be purified to the same quality. The infrastructure needed to purify water and to treat the waste water and sewage after use is expensive and environmentally-damaging in resource and energy consumption.

In an ideal home, water would be re-used inside the house. A 'grey water' system would use waste water from the shower or washing machine to flush the toilet or to water the garden. The heat from waste hot water from the bath or the shower would go through a heat-recovery system to boost other household heating systems.

Even without such systems, there is plenty you can do to save water and energy.

The Bathroom Cabinet

Cosmetics and hygiene products are a continually growing market, forever being new and improved and forever being advertised on television. Shampoos, toothpaste, shaving foam, hairspray all come packaged in plastic, wasting resources and jeopardising health. Follow the guidelines on these pages, but more importantly, try and cut down on unnecessary products.

Packaging – Cosmetics and toiletries are often grossly over-packaged, with shampoo bottles packaged inside a box and toothpaste packed in complicated plastic tubes. Whatever you buy, check first to see if you can buy the same item in simpler and/or recyclable packaging. The Body Shop, for instance, sells shampoo and other products in re-fillable bottles.

Ingredients – Healthfood shops, and increasingly supermarkets and chemists, sell toiletries made from 'natural' ingredients. However, just because something is natural does not necessarily mean that it is safe and non-polluting – asbestos is a natural product. Buying cruelty-free cosmetics and toiletries made from vegetable-based ingredients, however, should avoid products with artificial ingredients and possible allergens, such as perfumes or colourings. 'Natural' products will often have simpler packaging.

The Bathroom Cabinet

Soap – Don't buy shower gel or liquid soap in bottles, no matter how environmentally friendly or natural the ingredients. A bottle runs out more quickly than a bar of soap and so works out more expensive, and uses far more packaging. Buy pure soap which has not been tested on animals. Pure soaps are unlikely to contain artificial colourings or perfumes, and will be made from vegetable-based ingredients. By washing with a flannel you will use less soap. Stick the small leftover pieces of soap onto your next bar, or save them and mix them with boiling water in a jar to make a soapy paste to use for general cleaning around the house.

Shampoo – The Body Shop sells shampoos made from vegetable-based ingredients in re-fillable bottles. Buying large bottles saves money as well as packaging. Look for cruelty-free shampoos whenever you can, avoiding overpackaged products, such as bottles inside boxes inside cellophane. Use as little shampoo as possible, if your whole head is covered in lather, you are probably using too much. If you wash your hair regularly, then you won't need two applications each time.

Flannels – A washable cotton flannel is better than buying a sea sponge, which is taken from the sea disturbing natural habitats. Sponges eventually fall apart and have to be replaced, whereas flannels can be made out of old towels that might otherwise be thrown away.

Deodorant – Don't buy deodorants or anti-perspirants in aerosol cans. Roll-on deodorants use less packaging and last longer. Deodorants and anti-perspirants involve continually putting chemicals on your skin, and so it is better to use them as little as possible. Most people don't need to wear them every day, for instance. Natural product catalogues and health food shops often sell alternatives to brand-named deodorants, although they can be expensive.

see Shaving Products page 113

see Gender Benders page 74

Shaving Foam – The best shaving foam to buy is a cream in a bowl which you lather yourself with a brush. This is available for both men and women. You get far more shaves from one bowl than from a spray can, saving packaging and money. Avoid aerosols – they are incredibly wasteful in packaging, they encourage you to use far more foam than you need and potentially they contain hormone disrupting chemicals. Shaving gel is marginally better than foam because it is more concentrated. Buy vegetable-based products and look for shaving bowls with refills – these are available from some high street shops as well as by mail order. Make sure your shaving brush is not made from animal hairs.

see Batteries page 108

Razors – Never buy disposable razors. Instead look for razors with replaceable and more durable blades. These also tend to be better for your skin. An electric shaver makes environmental sense if well looked after and lasts a long time – but don't buy a battery-powered one. Instead, buy a rechargeable shaver that also works from the mains – but check first what the built-in batteries are made of. When you buy an electric shaver, check whether spare parts are easily available and how long the manufacturer's guarantee lasts. The most common problem with electric shavers is the guard over the blade breaking and only certain makes sell replacements.

see Nailbrushes page 111

Nailbrushes – Avoid plastic brushes in favour of proper wooden ones with natural fibre bristles. These are available in high street shops, but you can also order them from Friends of the Earth, where both the wood and the bristles are made from sustainable sources.

The Bathroom Cabinet

Parts of Madagascar are under threat from mining companies who want to extract the island's white sands to make, amongst other products, toothpaste whitener. This mining threatens to destroy the local rainforests, the marine ecosystems and fishing grounds.

Toothpaste – Toothpaste used to come tinned as a powder – normally bicarbonate of soda – into which you would dip your wet toothbrush to make into a paste. These tins lasted for months. Later, toothpaste came in tubes, first made from metal and then plastic. Now, many toothpastes come in plastic pump-action containers, using even more plastic than before for the same amount of paste. The oil-based chemicals and artificial flavours, sweeteners and colourings contained in commercial toothpastes are potentially hazardous. Vegetable-based alternatives avoid this.

Don't buy toothpaste in pump-action tubes and look for brands made from vegetable-based ingredients. Toothpaste adverts on television encourage us to put paste along the length of the brush. This is far too much as you only need a pea-sized amount. Most toothpaste companies have at least one brand containing bicarbonate of soda - an alternative to shop-bought makes is to make your own from real bicarbonate of soda. This tastes strange until you get used to it – add peppermint oil for a more familiar flavour.

see Toothbrushes page 114

Toothbrushes – You can buy toothbrushes with replaceable heads, probably the best way of saving resources. Avoid electric toothbrushes – the heads still need to be replaced *and* they consume energy every time you brush your teeth. Make sure you don't buy toothbrushes packed inside heavy plastic boxes using more plastic than the brush itself. Save your old toothbrush for cleaning, e.g. bicycle chains.

Dental Floss – Reduce plastic and packaging by buying floss on a roll rather than individual floss strips on plastic handles. If possible, avoid buying flavoured dental floss because of the artificial chemicals they contain.

Sanitary Products

Over 3000 million sanitary towels and tampons are disposed of each year in the UK.

75% of blocked drains are caused by sanitary products.

Sanitary protection products are made up of a mixture of wood pulp, cotton, plastic and rayon. Producing and bleaching the fibres to make the majority of sanitary products involves the use of chlorine bleach, which ends up polluting the atmosphere, water and ultimately the user, as small quantities of chlorine remain in the product to be absorbed into the body. Chlorine in tampons is the cause of Toxic Shock Syndrome, which affects up to 17 women a year in the USA. The organic parts of sanitary products eventually break down when released into the environment, but the plastic backings never do. Never flush sanitary products down the toilet, regardless of what the manufacturers state on the packet.

Contact the Women's Environmental Network for more details on sanitary protection. see page 138

To make tampons and other sanitary products needs vast amounts of wood, requiring large areas of woodland to be cleared. Demand for sanitary products is continually increasing, putting more pressure on the world's forests and creating more pollution.

Sanitary products will soon be available with the EU Eco-Label.

Choose towels with minimum packaging and avoid individually wrapped products. Look for products which have not been bleached with chlorine and those without plastic liners or applicators. More and more products are being advertised as being for everyday use, whether you need them or not. Avoid using tampons between periods and don't use other sanitary products unless you really need to, despite what the advertising might say.

see Sanitary Products page 113

Washable Sanitary Towels – Advances are being made in sanitary products that can be used over and over again with maximum convenience and minimum environmental impact. They can be washed in the washing machine with a normal load, saving both resources and money.

Gender Benders

Hormone Disrupting Compounds (HDCs) are chemicals which the human (or animal) body mistakes for its own hormones. Because the body is sensitive to minute quantities of hormones, even extremely low concentrations of HDCs can disrupt natural functions.

HDCs are linked to a wide variety of diseases and medical problems in humans and animals. Between 1945 and 1990 the average male sperm count fell by 45%, while hormone-sensitive cancers of the breast, uterus, prostate and testes rose. Cancers and tumours have been found in fish and mammals in America's Great Lakes. Reproductive deformities have been seen in species as far apart as alligators in Florida, fish in the North Sea and otters in Britain. Immune system deficiencies have caused devastating epidemics among harbour seals in the North Sea and dolphins in the Mediterranean. In animals, these diseases have been linked to eating diets of fish contaminated at very low concentrations. Long term exposure to HDCs, from food, packaging and cosmetics, is held responsible for many immune deficiency problems in humans.

Phthalates – These chemicals are widely used in plastics and also found in vinyl flooring, emulsion paint and printing inks. Recent studies have found phthalates in foods and baby milk formula.

Alkylphenolic Compounds (APCs) – These are used in industrial detergents for wool washing and metal finishing, paints, agrochemicals and as a spermicidal lubricant on condoms. They are also found in some common shampoos and shaving foams (often not mentioned on the ingredients list). The most common APCs are nonoxynols and octoxynols.

Bisphenol A – This is used in lacquers to coat metal products such as food cans, bottle-tops and water supply pipes. It has been found in canned vegetables and in certain coatings used for plastic tooth fillings.

Organochlorine Pesticides – DDT is no longer used in the west but is still found in developing countries. Lindane and Attrazine are still allowed in the UK, despite being banned in other parts of the world.

Polychlorinated Biphenyls (PCBs) and Dioxins – PCBs are used as heat transfer fluids in transformers. Dioxins can be produced during activities such as incineration, paper manufacture and chlorinated chemical production.

Avoiding Gender Benders

Over fifty HDCs have been identified to which we are exposed to daily from food packaging, plastics, drinking water, the air and the food chain. They are present in shampoo, hair colourants, mousses, styling gels, shaving foams and in lubricants for condoms.

From January 1998, under European law, all cosmetics must list their main ingredients, which will make it easier for consumers to avoid potentially dangerous chemicals. Avoid products which contain nonoxynols such as nonoxynol-9, nonoxynol-4 sulphate, and octoxynols, e.g. octoxynol-30.

Elsewhere, HDCs are harder to avoid. You might stop buying milk in plastic bottles to avoid phthalates only to find that the glass bottles have been washed with APC detergents. If you cannot tell if a product or packaging contains HDCs write to the manufacturers or ring their freephone customer number and ask.

Contact Friends of the Earth Scotland for an up-to-date list of products not to buy. see page 121

Buying simpler and more environmentally-conscious products will help you to avoid HDCs, and is another reason for taking care in what you choose. Buy organic vegetables when you can and when you can't, wash and peel everything carefully, discarding the outer leaves of cabbage and lettuce. Avoid food packaging containing PVC, which environmental organisations world-wide, including Friends of the Earth, are campaigning to have phased out completely.

Saving Water

A dripping tap can leak up to four litres an hour, wasting up to 35m^3 a year. Make sure none of your taps leak and always replace worn washers. A dripping hot tap can waste 31 hot tanks a year. Never leave the water running unnecessarily. Brushing your teeth with the tap running, for instance, can waste 4.5 litres (one gallon) of water.

Fit water-efficient spray taps, or fit sprays to your existing ones. If you are re-fitting your bathroom, buy mixer taps for the basin and the bath which mix the water to the right temperature, using the minimum amount. Some of these taps switch themselves off automatically, saving even more water.

A Shower is Better Than a Bath – A bath uses around 170 litres (37 gallons) of water, compared to 80 litres (17 gallons) for a five minute shower. Showering every two days instead of having a bath saves 17,000 litres (3,640 gallons) a year, or 154 tanks of hot water, assuming no cold water is used.

If you don't have a shower, you can buy rubber attachments which fit on to the bath or basin taps and although not as good as a real shower, they are still effective, convenient and cheap. A special bath tap is available which converts into a shower head and can be hung on a wall. Don't have a shower or bath just to wash your hair.

Flushing the Toilet – Most toilets use over ten litres (two gallons) per flush, far more than is needed. Only flush when you need to and never just for a piece of tissue paper. If the toilet carries on flushing long after everything has disappeared, too much water is being used. Use less by putting a full plastic bottle inside the cistern. A water-saving toilet has a smaller cistern than normal toilets and a dual-flush system for using different amounts of water according to need. Dual-flush cisterns can be bought separately and fitted to your existing toilet. Never flush sanitary protection, it should be wrapped and thrown in the bin.

Saving Energy

Saving hot water always saves energy, but there are other ways to reduce energy consumption and use it more efficiently.

If you have an immersion heater (gas or electric), it can be hard to judge how much hot water is needed each day and inevitably some is wasted. This is particularly true in busy or large households when there might be five showers one day and none the next, but a tank of water may still have been heated. An electric shower only heats water as it is used, cutting down on the waste of heating unwanted hot water, and can be fitted without changing the rest of your hot water system. If you already have an electric shower, make sure you are not heating water unnecessarily in the immersion tank. You could also consider a gas condensing boiler, which also heats water on demand.

see Energy page 67

Ventilation – The most environmentally-friendly way to ventilate your bathroom is to open the window, especially when you are having a bath or a shower. Better than electric extractor fans, wind operated ones can be fitted into windows. These work by using the difference in air pressure between the inside and the outside, using no electricity at all.

Many bathrooms and toilets, especially in flats and tenements, have electronic extractor fans which come on automatically with the light and stay on for a while after. These fans are useful for preventing condensation but may be on more often than necessary, e.g. when you are brushing your teeth or combing your hair. If the fan comes on with the light, see whether it is possible to have it connected to its own switch so that you can control when it comes on. There may be planning regulations covering this. If you have a separate light above the sink, use that instead of the main light. In bathrooms or toilets with windows, open them rather than switching the fan on.

If you have an extractor fan in your bathroom or toilet, make sure the door is well draught-proofed, otherwise air from the rest of the house is sucked outside through the bathroom.

The Living Room

The living room, with the television, video, stereo and other appliances, and heating, is heavy on energy consumption, especially during the winter. Improved insulation and controllng heating systems better should lower fuel bills, reduce energy, and keep your room warmer.

see DIY pages 96-104

The carpet and decorating materials in the living room, as with all the rooms in the home, have an impact on the environment and, potentially, on your health. When re-decorating choose environmentally-sounder products such as natural fibre carpets or vegetable and water-based paints. Cutting down on indoor air pollution is just as important as reducing the environmental impact of what you buy.

see Greener Cleaning pages 48-50

Cleaning and dusting the living room has environmental consequences and pages 48 to 50 give details of greener alternatives. Keeping a room well-ventilated by frequently opening the windows helps reduce asthma problems, aggravated by dust mites. This is particularly important if you have small children, pets and rooms containing lots of soft furnishing and thick carpets.

If your living room is on the ground floor and faces south, then you might have a conservatory. Conservatories trap the sun's heat and even in the middle of the winter can be quite warm on a sunny day. Opening the doors to the conservatory on sunny days lets the warmth into the house and even on cold days it acts as an extra layer of protection against the cold. Make sure the conservatory floor is well insulated and fit blinds to protect against the sun in the summer. Conservatories are available made from wood instead of PVC: look for sustainably sourced timber.

see PVC page 31
see Timber page 103

Even without a conservatory, a sunny room can trap the sun's heat and circulate it around the house. Leave the door open whenever the sun is shining and turn down the heating accordingly.

Televisions and Electronic Equipment

Fashion and technology bring with them endless developments, making us continually update and replace our electronic and audio-visual equipment. Making the situation worse is the fact that many products cannot be repaired once they are broken and instead need to be replaced. The environmental priority when dealing with televisions, hi-fis, radios and all other electronic equipment, is to make the most of what you already have in the house. Look after it, have it repaired if possible and only replace it as a last resort.

Standby Mode – A lot of audio-visual equipment has a standby mode, meaning that even when it is switched off it consumes electricity. For items such as televisions with a remote control, the standby lets you switch on and off from a distance. Use the real on/off switch and never leave it on standby over night. Even without remote controls, stereos and hi-fis can have a standby mode. With pre programmable digital radios, a continual supply of electricity is needed to store the radio settings, and some makes even come equipped with batteries as a backup should there be a power cut. The only way for these types of stereo to not consume power is for them to be switched off at the wall. Don't put batteries in. As with all the minuscule amounts of electricity that get consumed around the house, everything mounts up.

see Batteries page 108

Tapes, CDs And Records – The most resource-efficient way of getting hold of tapes, records and CDs is to borrow them. Public libraries have records and tapes, and video shops hire films and computer games.

Personal Computers – If you are buying new computer equipment, look for the Energy Star rating. This scheme is administered by the American Government, but it covers many products sold in this country. For products made in this country, ask about energy consumption when you are buying. Make sure you switch items such as printers and monitors off overnight and when not being used for long periods, using the switch on the wall if you have to.

see Recycling page 112

Recycling – Contact the Recycling Advisory Group for Scotland for details of electronics recycling in your area. Most electronic equipment can be recycled where the facilities exist.

Energy Saving Bulbs

The most common type of lighting, the filament bulb, was invented a century ago and has hardly changed since, despite massive leaps in technology. The filament bulb is extremely inefficient, only 10% of the energy it uses is turned into light, the rest is converted into heat. Most normal lightbulbs can be replaced by energy efficient varieties, which give off the same amount of light for a lot less energy.

A compact flourescent bulb uses less than a quarter of the energy of a normal bulb.

Compact Fluorescent Lightbulbs – These last eight times longer than normal bulbs and use only a quarter of the energy. Over its lifetime, an energy-efficient bulb saves between £20 and £50 and although costing around £10 each to buy, it pays for itself in its first year. The main differences between compact fluorescent bulbs and their counterparts are that they take a few seconds to warm up when first switched on and the light they give off may vary slightly, depending upon the make and the type of lampshade. These differences are only slight and you should soon get used to them.

Most compact fluorescent bulbs are designed as direct replacements for normal bulbs, but for even greater energy savings special light fittings can be bought which need specialised bulbs. Fluorescent bulbs need a special control starter to make them work, which is built into normal CFL bulbs, making them heavier. Specialised fittings already include an electronic starter, which makes the bulbs lighter, more energy efficient and cheaper. If you are considering replacing entire light sockets, fit fluorescent fittings.

Filament bulb	CFL
100W	20W
75W	15W
60W	11W

Equivalent energy consumption of normal and energy saving bulbs.

Where to Fit Fluorescent Bulbs – Wherever a light is left on for four hours or more, it is worth fitting energy-saving bulbs. Less than four hours, the energy savings are too low to warrant the added expenditure of a new bulb. The kitchen, the living room, the landing, anywhere the lights are left on for long periods of time are places you can make huge energy savings by replacing the lightbulbs. Fluorescent bulbs come in a variety of shapes and fittings, suitable for most existing light sockets, including table lamps. Some lampshades and fittings are too small for the new bulbs, which tend to be bigger and heavier than normal bulbs.

Where Not to Fit Fluorescent Bulbs – Don't put fluorescent bulbs in toilets, cupboards or rooms you rarely use. To save energy in these rooms, fit lower wattage bulbs. Compact fluorescent bulbs cannot be used with dimmer switches or certain other electronic or timer controls and shouldn't be fitted in automatic presence detectors, which usually don't switch lights on long enough to save much energy in any case.

Strip Lights – Kitchens and bathrooms often have fluorescent strip lights, which are even more energy-efficient than compact fluorescent bulbs. Old strip lights are usually 38mm in diameter and are less efficient than the more modern 26mm diameter ones. These should still fit into your strip light socket, unless it is very old (in which case it should be replaced any way as modern ones are themselves more efficient). Strip lights should not be left on all the time.

Lighting

As well as fitting energy-efficient bulbs, you can reduce your energy consumption by using less light and using it more efficiently.

Using Less Light – We don't use lighting just to see with, it is also part of a room's decoration, which is why we have table lamps, spot-lights, side lamps and so on to create different lighting effects. Don't switch all the lights on at once - just the ones you need. If several light bulbs are controlled from the same switch, you often end up putting on more lights than you need. Think about taking out some of the bulbs - you can always put them back when needed.

Using Light Efficiently – A bright side lamp (with an energy-efficient bulb) can replace two other lights. If you're watching television, you don't need as much light as when you're reading, for instance. Make sure lighting is directed to where you need it. Equipment to help lower your energy consumption is available, but not always compat-ible with energy-efficient light bulbs:

Movement Detector Switches – These cost around £23 and are easily fitted. These activate the light when somebody walks into the room, thus consuming energy only when needed. This works well in certain situations: instead of leaving the landing light on overnight if you have children, for instance, with a movement sensor it will come on automatically when a door is opened, and go off again after a fixed period of no movement. They can be overridden and used as normal light switches. Unfortunately, low-energy bulbs cannot be used with these fittings, but the energy savings should compensate for this. You can use movement sensors outside with normal bulbs, as security lighting or to replace an outside light which would otherwise be on permanently.

Timer Plugs – These allow you to control the times an appliance is in use. If, for security reasons, you leave a light on when you go out, fit a timer plug to a lamp and set it to go on and off at certain times, instead of leaving it on constantly. This is particularly useful if you go on holiday.

Radiators

If you have central heating, inefficient use of radiators wastes energy and doesn't heat your home properly. Don't put furniture in front of radiators – this stops the warm air from circulating around the room. Air trapped in a radiator stops it from heating efficiently, so make sure you bleed them all regularly. A bleeding key can be bought from most hardware and ironmonger shops.

see Radiator Insulation Panels page 112

Foil Reflector Panels – An energy-efficient radiator has a foil lining on the wall behind it to reflect the heat back into the room. This is especially vital when the radiator is against an outside wall. Paste kitchen silver foil on the wall, shiny side facing the room, using wallpaper paste or flour and water, or buy purpose-made foil with grooves to encourage an upwards air flow.

Wooden Shelves – Fit wooden shelves above your radiators. This forces the warm air to circulate round the room instead of going straight up the wall to the ceiling. If the radiator is under a window, the shelf stops the heat from going straight up behind the curtains, the bottoms of which should meet the shelf.

Individual Thermostats – Radiators running from a central heating system should have individual thermostatic controls on them, fitted onto the hot water in-flow pipe. These allow you to control the temperature in each room, and save heating empty rooms or over-heating rooms which are already warm enough. If your radiators don't already have these, consider having them fitted. They are reasonably cheap, you can install them yourself and will pay for themselves in saved energy costs. Make sure you use them to control the temperature in each room, setting them at low or off altogether in empty rooms. Don't put thermostats on radiators in rooms with a room thermostat.

Storage Heaters

Storage heaters can use up vast amounts of energy if not used effectively so they must be kept under strict control. Storage heaters have no central control and so can be operated individually. They heat up during the night, storing the heat in bricks for gradual release during the day. These types of heater are designed to be left on all night to make use of cheaper off-peak electricity, but there is still scope for energy saving. Keep all radiators clear of obstructions and any furniture that stops the warm air circulating around the room.

To switch off a heater completely, it must be turned off at the wall. Most storage heaters have two controls, an input and an output. Some are fitted with boosters.

Input – This controls the charge overnight. Setting it on low reduces the amount of energy used, but if not enough heat is stored during the night then it won't be there in the day unless your heaters are fitted with boosters. As the weather gets warmer, it is important to turn these down. In toilets and other rooms that do not need to be as warm as the rest of the building, turn down the input control as a matter of course. Turning the input control up or down during the day will have no effect on temperature.

The booster control switches on an electric heater which consumes a vast amount of energy, much more than the radiator normally uses during the night.

Output – This opens and closes the flap at the top of the heater, allowing the heat to escape. The more it is open, the more heat is released. Some heaters have fans and boosters to produce more heat. Since the electricity will have been consumed already during the night, there is not much potential for energy saving, other than to resist using the booster unless really necessary. It is important to close the flaps overnight otherwise all the heat is released straight away, leaving none for the daytime.

Solid Fuel Fires

Many homes have open fires, although in many urban areas there may be controls on the fuels allowed. In smokeless zones, only smokeless fuels can be used. These fuels burn at a very high temperature, giving off minimal smoke. Elsewhere, where there are no restrictions, open fires, room heaters and stoves can burn wood, coal and peat. If you read lots of papers, buy a log-making machine which squashes soaked newspapers into bricks which then burn for up to an hour.

see Log Makers
page 111

All types of solid fuel fire need plenty of air so don't over-insulate the rooms they are in against draughts.

Open Fires – These are not very efficient as a lot of the heat goes straight up the chimney, but more modern grates let you regulate the heat, making it burn more efficiently. If you regularly use an open fire, it is worth considering the installation of a concealed back boiler which either heats a tank of water or runs up to eight radiators. This is the best way of maximising the heat from an open fire.

Room Heaters – These burn solid fuels inside a stove, sometimes with a boiler. These are far more efficient than open fires, converting more of the fuel to heat, and emitting more of the heat into the room. Fuel burns most efficiently when it is hottest. Room heaters will usually burn different types of fuel, including peat. For both open fires and room heaters, make sure the grate is kept clean to let the fire burn as hot as possible. The cleaner the grate, the easier it is to control the air flow and how hot the fire burns.

see Firelighters
page 110

Firelighters – Firelighters are usually made from paraffin and other flammable chemicals. Save twigs, kindling and screwed up newspapers instead of buying firelighters.

Windows

20% of a house's heat loss is through uninsulated windows.

Curtains and Blinds – The thinner the curtains, the more heat they let through. Line curtains with thermal lining, available from curtain and upholstery shops. Close them at night in the winter, and even during the day if the room is not in use. If there is a radiator under the window, make sure the curtain is tucked behind it or that it sits on the sill. Stiff roller blinds fitted close to the windows are also effective as insulation, especially in conjunction with curtains.

see Radiators page 83

Shutters – If your home is older, you may have interior, fold-out wooden shutters, common in many tenements. These are good insulators, against noise as well as cold. Unfortunately, they were out of fashion for a while and many people had them removed or painted over. If yours still work, clear any obstructions and use them, especially in winter. If you have shutters, but they have been painted over, renovate them or have them replaced.

DIY Double Glazing – Double glazing options range from plastic sheeting to complete replacement windows. You can buy kits of plastic sheets and sticky tape, but clingfilm is just as effective. Stick it firmly round the edges of the windows and blow a hairdryer over the plastic until the creases have disappeared. This is very effective as an instant option, the only drawback being that it is awkward to open the windows once the plastic is in place but, if it is taken down properly, the plastic can be re-used. This works well if you are renting.

Secondary Double Glazing – This slots into existing window frames, and is easy to dismantle. It is cheaper than replacing your existing windows and in conservation areas you may not be able to replace your windows at all, making this your only option. Don't buy PVC-framed glazing.

Replacement Double Glazing – Because replacement double glazing is expensive, it should only be considered as a long term project or when your original windows are in need of repair. Take all other insulation measures first. Double glazing also keeps out noise, so living near a busy road might make this more of a priority. Most commercially available double glazing, however, uses PVC and alternatives are hard to find. Ask for double glazing frames using wood, metal or more environmentally-friendly plastics.

see Windows page 115

se PVC page 31

The Bedroom

We spend over a third of our lives in the bedroom, mostly asleep. Children, particularly those doing homework, students and people in shared accommodation spend even longer here. Our clothes, bed-clothes, duvets, curtains, and carpets all have environmental and health consequences.

see DIY pages 96-101

Non-toxic – Because we spend so much time in the bedroom, it is important to try to limit exposure to artificial chemicals linked to health problems and allergies, notably asthma. Non-allergenic fabrics and fillings are available, made from natural products and dyes. Try to buy paints and other materials, such as carpets, which are as non-toxic as possible.

see pages 80-86

Energy-efficiency – Comparatively, little energy is consumed in the bedroom, and this is mainly for heating and lighting, where savings are possible. If any light, including desk and table lamps, is on for more than four hours a day, fit energy saving bulbs.

Toys – Avoid cheap plastic toys which break easily or will go out of fashion quickly. Swap toys with family, friends and neighbours. When the children out-grow their toys, pass them on to younger ones.

Clothes

Buy Less – The fashion industry encourages us to buy new clothes every season with the result that many of us have wardrobes full of rarely-worn clothes. Try not to buy more clothes than you need.

Have your shoes repaired and re-soled before they are too damaged or worn to be mended.

Repair Old Clothes – Repair clothes whenever you can. Most rips and tears can be patched or repaired, making clothes last a lot longer than they otherwise would. Patched jeans can last for ages and other old and repaired clothes, even if they aren't hugely fashionable, can still be worn on plenty of occasions.

Second Hand – Second hand and charity shops are a good source of cheap and reasonable quality clothing – it's not all flares and tank tops. This saves money and resources, and the proceeds go to charity. Just as important as buying from second hand shops is to donate them your old clothes.

New Clothes – Buy good quality clothing which will last a while before falling apart or going out of fashion. Beware of false economies – a cheap T-shirt may seem like a bargain at the time, but it will probably shrink or run in the wash, ruining other clothes. Avoid clothes which need to be washed separately or at different temperatures from the rest of your clothes. Look for the EU Eco-Label.

An estimated £30,000,000,000 worth of unused clothing hangs in British wardrobes.

Recycling – The best way of getting rid of good quality clothes is to give them to a charity shop, either directly or via a textile recycling bank. Organisations, such as Oxfam, re-sell the best items sending the rest for humanitarian relief. Unusable clothing is taken apart and the fibres recycled.

Bedclothes

see Asthma page 92

While we are asleep, we are particularly vulnerable to toxins from bedding which has been chemically treated and artificially dyed. Dust mites, linked asthma and allergies, also thrive in the warm conditions.

Artificial Chemicals – Formaldehyde is a common chemical, used in carpets, foam fillings, plastic flooring, chipboard and in artificial and treated fibres. Formaldehyde, other solvents and vapours from chemicals can all cause skin and eye irritation and dryness, headaches and sore throats. Individually, in small amounts, these chemicals are not a major hazard, but together throughout the home, their impact begins to mount up. Research indicates that the air inside the home is ten times more polluted with solvents than outside. Because we spend so much time wrapped up in bed, it is particularly important to have chemical-free bedclothes.

see Bedlinen page 108

Fabrics advertised as 'easy care' or 'iron free' will have been treated with formaldehyde to prevent them creasing when they are washed. Choose bedding which is undyed and unbleached, or dyed with natural mineral and vegetable dyes. If you cannot find unbleached fabrics, look for those which have been bleached with hydrogen peroxide rather than chlorine. To reduce the impact of chemicals in your existing bedding, wash it regularly at a hot temperature and dry it on the line, not in a tumble dryer.

A hot water bottle uses much less energy than an electric blanket. Alternatives to rubber hot water bottles include thick glass bottles wrapped in a towel or wheat bed warmers.

see Natural Fibres page100-101

Natural Fibres – You can buy bedclothes made from natural fibres and fillings. Pillows, mattresses and duvets are often filled with polyester foams; sheets, pillowcases and duvet covers are often made from nylon, polyester and other artificial fibres. Apart from the fact that these materials are made from non-renewable petrochemical products, they are a potential health hazard. Choosing natural alternatives to these materials avoids many of the problems described above and uses products made from renewable resources, although feathers and hair may cause allergies.

Recycled Fibres – You can buy duvets and pillows filled with recycled polyester plastic material made from recycled bottles. This is a much better option for the environment than buying non-recycled artificial fibres.

Babies

Nappies – A baby gets through dozens of nappies every week, and in most families this normally means disposable ones. Nearly three billion disposable nappies are thrown away every year, ending up in landfill sites, where they take tens of years to rot down. Not only must all these nappies be disposed of, they consume huge amounts of resources to be made in the first place. Disposable nappies are made of paper and plastic. They are bleached and contain various chemicals including perfumes and dyes (pink for girls, blue for boys). Contact the Women's Environmental Network for further information on environmental aspects of bringing up children.

see Nappies page 111

Towelling nappies are not really an option for most people compared with the ease and convenience of disposable ones, but there are other alternatives. Washable, waterproof elasticated cotton nappies and accessories can be bought by mail order and from specialist shops, together with flushable paper liners and cotton nursing pads. Although the greener alternatives may require more effort than their disposable counterparts, large savings can be made, both financial and environmental. As ever, it is often convenience that heralds environmental damage.

2,877,000,000 disposable nappies were thrown away in 1991.

Hygiene – Disposable convenience products, such as wet wipes and other baby products, are usually over-packaged and made with chemical perfumes and preservatives. Try to avoid unnecessary products in favour of simpler alternatives (such as soap and water). See if you can do without before you buy a new product and choose products which have not been tested on animals.

Over 20,000,000 packets of disposable baby wipes are bought and thrown away each year.

Small babies are big consumers. Cots, prams, toys and clothes are all outgrown alarmingly quickly yet, encouraged by advertising most parents buy these new - at least for their first child. Try to use hand-downs from friends and family. You don't need to spend money to be a good parent – don't be tempted into wanton consumerism by the birth a new baby.

Asthma

The number of childhood asthma and hay fever sufferers has doubled over the past 25 years.

There are around 300,000 asthma sufferers in Scotland, and across the UK the condition kills 2000 people each year. There is no single cause of asthma. Instead a number of pollutants combine to make people more susceptible, the main source being vehicle exhaust fumes. In the home, central heating, poor ventilation caused (ironically) by better insulation and double glazing, carpets, fabrics, and washing clothes at lower temperature all create ideal conditions for dust mites to breed, especially where damp is a problem.

Scottish hospital admissions for asthma have more than doubled in the last decade - 10,000 people were admitted to hospital in 1990.

Microscopic dust mites breed in mattresses, bedding, carpets, curtains and upholstery. They feed on human skin scales, making them more of a problem in beds. The dust mites' droppings trigger asthma – during a mite's three month life span, it lays 20 to 40 eggs and produces up to 2000 droppings.

In Sweden, where building standards dictate that all homes are triple glazed, asthma is increasing and is a major concern. This increase is being linked to reduced ventilation because of the high standard of triple glazing. Taking steps to tackle dust mites, even if you are not affected yourself, will help relieve other minor respiratory complaints and generally contribute to a healthier lifestyle.

Washing – Regularly washing bedclothes, curtains, seat covers and other fabrics at high temperatures helps kill dust mites and their eggs. Regular washing, and drying on the line, reduces dust and loose particles in fabrics. This is particularly important for bedclothes. Always wash new bedclothes before sleeping in them. Boilable pillows, duvets and cushions are available, although these tend to be made from polyethylene. Air bedclothes between washes.

Freezing – Freezing also kills dust mites and is particularly recommended for children's soft toys. A young child may not like the idea of their favourite teddy being shut in the freezer overnight, but if you seal it tightly in a plastic bag, it won't go soggy when you defrost it. Sometimes you have to be cruel to be kind!

Ventilation and Heating – The energy-saving recommendations concerning insulation may well contribute to reducing natural ventilation, which is vital for health. Ensure that all rooms, especially bedrooms, are not over-heated, and are regularly well ventilated. Open all the windows fully once a week to blast fresh air through the house (with the heating switched off), and sleep with bedroom windows slightly open. Cooking with gas aggravates asthma, so cook with the kitchen window open and ensure the window is well ventilated.

see Bedlinen page 108

see Natural Fibres pages 100-101

Fabrics – If asthma is a particular problem in your family, you can take steps to reduce your exposure further. Dust mite-proof mattress covers and pillowcases are available from high street shops and specialist suppliers. Alternatives to carpet limit areas where dust mites breed and are healthier, as well as being better for the environment.

Elsewhere, regular hoovering, drying clothes on the line, damp dusting as well as avoiding artificial cleaning products and household items (e.g. chipboard) all help to control dust and dust mites, reduce your exposure to artificial chemicals and limit the chances of asthma in your family. For those who suffer from severe asthma, face masks are available for indoor and outdoor use.

Tobacco And Cigarettes

Cigarette smoke is the major source of indoor air pollution in the western world. It contains about 4000 chemicals including carcinogens, irritants and toxic gases.

Cigarette smoke also contains two greenhouse gases: CO_2 and methane. World-wide, smoking generates about 2.6 billion kg of CO_2 each year and 5.2 billion kg of methane.

Smoking is bad for your health: both the health of the smoker and everyone in the vicinity. The average smoker spends £980 per year on smoking so if you smoke, and the financial and health reasons do not prompt you to give up, then there are compelling environmental reasons to quit the weed.

Tobacco is one of the most widely-grown, non-food crops, occupying large tracts of land, usually in developing countries. One study estimates that 10-12 million people could be fed by the land currently growing tobacco. The tobacco plant is not very resistant to diseases and so requires huge amounts of chemical herbicides, pesticides as well as fertilisers, causing both pollution and ill-health. Many chemicals that are banned in developed countries are still used in many tobacco-growing states and farmers and their families are exposed to high levels of contamination with little or no protective clothing.

Drying and curing tobacco consumes inordinate quantities of wood: 123 cubic metres of wood is needed for every tonne of tobacco. Malawi, heavily deforested and dependant on imported wood, produces 35 000 tonnes of cured tobacco per year and around a quarter of all wood burned is used by the tobacco industry.

Every day in the UK, smokers throw away 200 million cigarette butts and 20 million cigarette packets, many of which end up outside.

The solution to environmental and health problems is very simple: *Give up*

DIY

Painting and Decorating

Solvents – Paints, varnishes, carpets, glues, fabrics and chipboard furniture are all sources of solvents. Solvents are used in manufacturing to keep chemicals in a liquid state until they need to dry. For paints, varnishes and glues, this means the solvents evaporate into your home as they dry. For foam fillings and linings, glues in chipboards and fabric dyes, the solvents will have dried long before reaching your home, but they continue to evaporate indefinitely. The smell of new carpets, lino and furniture is from solvents.

Solvents are linked with skin, nose, eye and throat irritations and are a major cause of sick building syndrome. Products made from natural renewable ingredients are safer and do not contain polluting and resource-consuming materials. Whatever products you buy, ensure they are solvent-free.

Paint – Paint production can be environmentally-damaging (chemicals used in paint manufacture include chlorine, cadmium, titanium dioxide (especially in white paint) and sulphuric dioxide). Heavy metals and other toxins used to colour and bond the liquids are themselves dangerous, polluting the environment and consuming energy during production. Dumping paint pots, especially the half empty ones is hazardous with toxins leaching out into the surrounding water table.

see Paints page 112

Natural pigment paints are just as effective as normal paints but without the environmental drawbacks. Various companies produce natural paints for general household use as well as outside masonry, woodwork and iron-work. These are made from natural pigments from plants and minerals, and natural oils and resins. A common ingredient in natural paints is shellac, the secretion of the lac insect, which bonds to form a solid surface. Unlike other paints, many mail order environmentally-aware paints are sold as kits which you mix yourself. This allows you to make up only as much as you need in the exact colour you want. Germany has been at the forefront in developing eco-friendly paints and most commonly-available brands in Germany meet consumer safety standards. Commercial paints are now available with the EU Eco-Label, but you should still check the ingredients and watch out for artificial chemicals.

Removing Paint – The least harmful way of stripping paint is to sand it down. Despite the energy consumption this is still preferable to using harmful paint stripping chemicals. The existing paintwork in your home may contain lead. Don't burn it off, wear a protective face mask and keep the room well ventilated. Throw the paint shavings away in a sealed container.

Varnishes and Wood Stains – Wood stains are an alternative to commercial paints. Rather than coating the wood in a uniform colour, they stain the wood, highlighting the natural grains whilst protecting and colouring it. Natural oils and resins protect the wood with fewer harmful consequences. Choose water-based varnishes made from shellac. Varnishes are covered by the EU Eco-Label.

Wallpaper – Many wallpapers are PVC vinyl-based and it is hard to find recycled wallpaper. You will have little or no choice over which dyes and other chemicals are used. Self adhesive wall coverings will invariably contain fungicides, which you should avoid as much as possible. Vinyl and plastic wallpapers seal the walls which stops them from breathing, which then requires fungicide. Wallpaper pastes often also contain fungicide, even though it isn't needed in most situations. Some large DIY shops will sell fungicide-free paste, but you may have to buy it by mail order. When you do need a fungicide use borax instead.

see Wallpaper Paste
page 115

Wood-chip paper and wallpaper lining is cheap and can be painted over in the colour of your choice. Although not necessarily made from waste products, these wallpapers use less resources than do other types and are longer-lasting in that they can be repainted instead of being replaced.

Flooring

When choosing a new floor covering, take into account the indoor pollution caused by artificial fibres and materials. You can get an idea of the problem from the smell of a new carpet or a new vinyl floor (volatile organic compounds from the solvents and fibres). Although the smell fades eventually gases continue to evaporate. Added to the other gases and compounds found in most homes, from chipboard furniture, upholstery, cleaning products, wallpapers and paints indoor air pollution becomes an ever-present hazard. As we live in ever more artificial environments (in offices, shops and banks as well as homes) it is important to reduce our exposure to risks whenever we can.

Most carpets and vinyls are made from petrochemical-based synthetics manufactured from non-renewable resources. As such they are not biodegradable, and are difficult to recycle, given the complex mixture of materials and fibres. The only other disposal options for discarded carpet are landfilling or incineration.

see PVC page 31

Vinyl linoleum, on a roll or in tiles, is a major source of PVC and should be avoided wherever possible. The use of PVC is strictly controlled in other countries as it is hazardous during manufacture, use and eventual disposal.

In Germany, half a million tonnes of textiles are sent to be landfilled every year. Plants are being built to recycle at least 90, 000 tonnes of carpet annually mainly back into new carpets.

Not all natural materials are problem-free, but you should be able to lay healthier and more environmentally-friendly floor coverings in your house at around the same price as usual carpets and tiles. Whatever floor material you choose for your home, first make sure that the floor is properly insulated against draughts and sound.

Wooden Flooring

Most homes already have wooden floorboards hidden beneath the carpet, needing little more than sanding and polishing to make a traditional wooden floor. Once polished, a wooden floor needs less cleaning than a carpet. Dust can be swept up, using no electricity, and dirt can be wiped off with a damp cloth. No matter how often you vacuum a carpet, dust always stays in the pile, whereas a rug on a wooden floor can be shaken outside and/or washed in the washing machine. The greenest, as well as the cheapest floor is your existing floorboards. If this is impossible in your home, fitting a new wooden floor on top of your existing floor is a relatively cheap option.

Sanding And Polishing – This is a straightforward, but admittedly messy, DIY job. You can hire a sander from a tool-hire shop and buy different coloured wood stains and polishes. This is generally cheaper than having a new floor installed. Use natural vegetable dyes to colour the grain of the wood and a water-based varnish to make the floor easy to clean with a damp cloth. Beeswax is a an even better choice, but makes the floor extremely slippery. To stop rugs and mats slipping stick them to the floor using strong tape or specially-made grips. Don't buy mats with non-slip backing as this is normally made of foam or plastic.

Research in Sweden comparing the environmental performance of floors made of wood, lino and vinyl found that on most counts wood was the best option.

see Insulation page 104

A New Wooden Floor – If you have a concrete floor or floorboards that are too damaged to be sanded consider fitting a new wooden floor on top. Most large DIY chains sell wooden blocks which can be easily fitted onto most types of flooring. This is also the best solution if you need to insulate draughty or cold concrete floors. Where possible, make sure that the wood comes from renewable resources. Better still, see if you can find reclaimed wood such as from an old building being demolished. It is better to buy unvarnished or untreated wood, as you can then choose what chemicals you use to seal it. Order untreated wood direct from the manufacturers if you can't find it in the shops. Make sure your floor is well insulated before fitting new boards.

Natural Fibres and Materials

Natural fibre carpets and rugs come in a whole range of colours and textures with different kinds for different rooms. Because most natural fibres are grown and harvested in traditional ways, they do not threaten the environment; when eventually thrown away, they do not pollute and are bio-degradable. More shops are selling natural carpets and coverings. You can also buy them mail order.

Coir, sisal and jute can produce a rather rough-looking carpet compared to the more usual thick pile carpets, but when the fibres are died and woven with linen, wool or cotton the results are impressive. Natural fibre carpets last many times longer than their more polluting counterparts.

Make sure you don't buy a front door mat made from polypropylene.

Coir – Commonly made into doormats, coir comes from the husks of coconut shells, which would otherwise be thrown away. The fibres are spun into yarn and then woven into a range of products including rope and carpets which are 'faintly hairy and very hardy' according to one catalogue. Whatever you do, make sure that at least your doormat is made of coir rather than plastic

Sisal – Traditionally grown in Mexico, the plant's one metre long leaves are soaked until they disintegrate into tough fibres. Carpets and mats made of sisal are the most common and well-known of all the natural fibre floor coverings and come in a variety of textures and colours. The fibres are very hardwearing and long-lasting.

Jute – The fibres are extracted from the stem of the jute plant and made into a variety of products, including footwear, hessian cloths and sacks, wall coverings and as a natural replacement for foam in carpet backings as well as carpets and rugs themselves.

Cotton – Cotton is a natural fibre from the cotton plant. Although cotton is a common cash crop, requiring intensive agriculture and ususally depending on large inputs of artificial fertilizers and other chemicals, it is a more natural alternative to many of the other fibres available. Cotton fabrics are becoming increasingly available made from organic unbleached fibres, giving environmental and health benefits.

Wool – Although sheep farming can be environmentally-damaging when carried out on large scale, wool is essentially a renewable resource without the negative environmental and health consequences of artificial fibres. For clothing and soft furnishings around the house, use natural unbleached wool or products with natural dyes whenever possible.

see PVC page 31

see Flooring page 110

Linoleum (Marmoleum) – This is a traditional Scottish product made from powdered cork, linseed oil, wood resin, flour and chalk on a jute or hessian backing. Linoleum should not be confused with its imitation PVC lino and is available in rolls and tiles. It can be made to order with your own choice of pattern and colours.

Cork Tiles

see Cork page 119

Cork is an entirely natural product which comes from the bark of the cork oak tree. It is harvested every nine years without damaging the trees. In the intervening years, the trees are left to grow, supporting a rich diversity of wildlife. The land underneath the oak trees gets used for agriculture, mainly grazing, making the whole system productive and sustainable. The cork bark cannot be taken from trees less than 25 years old. The trees often grow for 150 years, guaranteeing forest cover in Mediterranean areas where deforestation is otherwise a problem. A natural product, cork is bio-degradable and does not pollute.

Cork floor tiles can be fitted wherever you might otherwise put vinyl and are a cheaper alternative to wooden floors, and are particularly suitable where the floor is damaged. Cork is made up of millions of tiny air pockets, which makes it perfect as an insulation material for sound as well as warmth.

Many supermarkets are introducing plastic 'corks' in bottles of wine. This threatens the whole cork industry as corks for bottling are its main product. Most other cork-based products, such as tiles, are made from the leftovers of 'real' corks.

Buying unvarnished cork tiles means you can choose the sealant. Water-based varnish and beeswax polish are two options. Polished cork is easy to clean with a damp cloth. Varnished cork is waterproof and good in the bathroom and the kitchen. Cork can also be stained in the colour of your choice. Damaged tiles can be replaced individually instead of having to re-do an entire room, so make sure you buy a few extra.

Use cork tiles on walls as insulation. Varnished, they make a good alternative to ceramic tiles in bathrooms, toilets and kitchens.

Timber and Windows

see PVC page 31

PVC – One of the consequences of the thinning ozone layer over the next half a century will be that the increased levels of ultra-violet light are set to damage PVC plastics used in construction. Many window frames are made of PVC, as are many window panes themselves. The UV rays will darken and eventually turn the plastic completely black, which is obviously not particularly useful in windows and conservatories. PVC is to be totally avoided. Choose glass for the panes and wood for the frames.

see Windows page 115

A fir tree plantation is no more a forest than a corn field is a meadow.

Mahogany is one of the most environmentally damaging sources of timber. It is a rare tree and yet much sought after. To get access to one mahogany tree results in many more being chopped down. Britain is the world's biggest importer of mahogany. Never buy anything made of mahogany.

Timber – Wood is the ultimate natural resource. Grown and harvested sustainably, forests can go on meeting human needs for fuel, timber and paper and still be natural habitats for a wide diversity of species of plant and animal. Vast expanses of land covered in one type of tree to be harvested at the same time, often replace old growth natural forests but do not support the same biodiversity of their natural predecessors. Clear felling forests leaves the soil suddenly exposed to wind and rain, resulting in severe soil erosion, and replacing them with tree monoculture kills natural wildlife and can acidify the ground and the water. In many parts of the world, cattle ranchers move in once the forests have been cleared.

The UK is one of the world's largest consumers of timber, using about 25 million cubic metres per year, more than the whole of India. Only 15% of what we use is actually grown here, even though Scotland used to be 95% forest. Most of our wood comes from Scandinavia, North America and Europe. In some parts of Finland, where 600 year-old trees are being felled, areas cleared in the 1960s are still totally barren. It is important that we find sustainable methods of growing timber and of recycling wood for re-use.

see Friends of the Earth page 150

Whenever you can, choose wood over other materials. Look for companies who sell timber bearing the Forest Stewardship Council symbol and buy or use local and recycled timber wherever possible. Look for European softwoods and hardwoods instead of wood from tropical sources. For a comprehensive guide to acceptable alternatives to most timber sources, read Friends of the Earth's Good Wood Guide. Recycling all your paper helps cut down the need for wood, as does having any wood you are throwing away recycled.

Insulation

Effective insulation is one of the most efficient ways of reducing your energy consumption and your home's contribution to carbon dioxide pollution. Insulating your home can be an expensive exercise and so should be considered as a long term measure unless it is a priority, if you have an uninsulated attic or loft. You should seek professional advice for major insulation jobs as unless proper precautions are taken, you may end up with condensation where internal walls touch outside ones. Whenever you are insulating, make sure that you do not block sources of ventilation.

see Insulation page 111

Materials – Both shredded paper (treated with fire retardant) and wool (which is naturally fire resistant) are ecologically sound materials for insulating. Using insulation made from recycled paper fibres uses only 2% of the energy needed for polyurethane-based insulation and 10% of that needed for insulation made from mineral fibres. The paper makes good use of a waste resource. Neither wool or paper contain formaldehyde or other artificial chemicals. In old buildings, ash was used under floors as soundproofing and insulation.

Roof Space – If you have an uninsulated attic, or if the insulation is less than 100 mm thick, make this a priority. Loft insulation should be at least 15 cm thick. If your water tank is in the attic, insulate over it, not under it as the heat from the house below helps stop it from freezing in the winter. Make sure all water pipes are insulated separately. If you have had your loft converted, insulate the top rafters, but make sure you leave a gap between the insulation and the roof itself for ventilation. If your joists or rafters are not tall enough to allow enough depth of insulation, add wooden slats to make them deeper.

External Walls – 30% of a home's heat is lost through the outside walls, making this the next most important priority for insulation. The most straightforward method is cavity wall insulation, for houses with unfilled cavity walls. This has to be carried out by professional contractors who inject the insulation through the outer wall. Covering the outer wall with an insulating layer is the most effective method of insulation as it keeps the heat in the entire building. This is a major job and has to be carried out professionally.

The cost will vary according to the size of your house. This is only really appropriate for houses and where the external façade needs to be re-surfaced.

Internal Walls – Where neither of the two above options are available to you, i.e. if you live in a tenement, your home is in a conservation area or you do not have cavity walls, consider insulating the interior surface of external walls. Attach rigid board insulation to external walls and then cover it with plaster board, some makes of which come pre-insulated. After this you just decorate as you would a normal wall. You will have to alter the architraving around doors and windows if you choose this type of insulation.

see flooring page 110

Flooring – Insulating solid floors and beneath wooden floor boards is a relatively straightforward, if messy and time consuming job. This is most appropriate on ground floors. For suspended wood floors, lift the floorboards and fill either with a solid or loos-fill insulation material, making sure you leave a gap below for ventilation. Netting or wooden slats will have to be fitted to support the insulation. The insulation material will have to be fitted above solid floors – consider using old carpets. Place timber battens across the floor with the insulation material between and then put your new wooden floor on top. Fill gaps under skirting boards with papier mache.

Batteries

A totally green battery would last forever, would not contain any toxic chemicals and does not exist. In anticipation of there ever being a totally green battery, we have to make do, which primarily means trying to go without as much as possible. Batteries contain a variety of toxic chemicals, most notably mercury. When incinerated, batteries produce highly dangerous fumes and leave toxic ash. Disposing of batteries in landfill leaks the chemicals into the environment. Look for mercury free batteries.

see Waste Disposal page 28

Avoid Batteries – Never use battery-operated appliances at home when they can be plugged into the mains, such as radios or electric shavers. Use extension leads to take radios outside into the garden. Wind up radios have recently been invented as a way of disseminating health education in the Third World and can be bought here. Although more expensive than a normal radio, for every one sold, two can then be sent to developing countries. For 25 seconds of winding, you get half an hour of electricity. Don't buy watches which need batteries, instead use old fashioned, but eco, wind up watches. Solar powered calculators, and increasingly other products, can be found.

see Friends of the Earth page 116

A battery uses up 50 times more energy to consume than it gives out in its lifetime.

Rechargeable Batteries – These are usually ni-cad batteries and so contain the toxic chemical cadmium. If you must use batteries, then the best option by far is to use rechargeable ones as they can be recharged as much as 500 times each, even if each individual charge does not last as long as a non-rechargeable type. Although they cost more to buy initially, they save you money in the medium term. Torches are available which plug directly into the wall and so are permanently charged up. Another alternative are wind up torches, although they are hard to find. When using rechargeable batteries, it is important to make sure that the batteries are totally dead before recharging them each time, and because they lose their charge very suddenly, they should not be used in smoke alarms.

Batteries will soon be available with the EU Eco-Label.

In Sweden, many trains are equipped with sockets for personal stereo headphones. The trains play radio stations and different kinds of music, in turn saving thousands of batteries every year.

Bicycle Lights – In Germany it is compulsory for all bicycles to have dynamos. These are infinitely more reliable and by far the greenest option for lighting your bicycle than batteries. For most other lights, except those taking AAA batteries, use rechargeable ones – but always carry fully-charged spares as they lose their charge faster than non-rechargeable types. Flashing LED lights are by far the most energy-efficient lights and use the smallest batteries.

see Local Authorities page 122

Recycling – It will soon be compulsory for local authorities to provide recycling facilities for batteries, as has already been the case for several years in many other European countries. Until the facilities exist, you could store your batteries somewhere cool in a tin. Button cell batteries, such as are found in hearing aids and some cameras, can sometimes be returned to retailers or surgeries.

Product Directory

Find the product or category you are looking for in the margin. Look up the address of the company in the addresses section.

Adhesives The Green Shop Catalogue

Air Freshener FoE Catalogue

Air Ioniser The Green Shop Catalogue

Aprons FoE Catalogue

Traidcraft

Baby Wear Products FoE Catalogue
washable nappy system, nursing pads, cot and pram blankets, body and play suits

The Green Shop Catalogue
nappies, washable liners

The Whole Thing Catalogue
mini-terry nappies

Design for a Healthy Environment
dust mite proof bedding

Bath Mats FoE Catalogue
unbleached cotton

Traidcraft
hand-woven, hand brushed cotton

Bathrobes FoE Catalogue
unbleached cotton

Design for a Healthy Environment
untreated cotton

Bathroom Products FoE Catalogue

The Green Shop Catalogue

Batteries and Battery Charger (mains and solar) The Green Shop Catalogue

Centre for Alternative Technology Catalogue

The Whole Thing Catalogue

FoE Catalogue

Bean Sprouter FoE Catalogue

The Whole Thing

Bedlinen FoE Catalogue
blankets, bedspreads, pillows, sheets, duvet covers

Northern Feather
quilts, pillows

Bedlinen (cont'd)

Design for a Healthy Environment
dust mite proof bedding , duvets, underblankets, sheets, cotton and wool blankets, mattress covers

Traidcraft (unbleached cotton, natural dyes)
duvets covers, sheets, pillowcases, bedspreads, throws

Beds

Alpha Beds
self assembly, futons, sofa-beds, mattresses

Design for a Healthy Environment
mattresses, solid pine and beech furniture

Airsprung Scotland

Beauty Products

FoE Catalogue
essential oils, balms, gels

The Green Shop Catalogue
cleansers, toners, scrubs, moisturisers, day and night creams

Montagne Jeunesse
products derived from plant extracts

The Body Shop

Brushes

FoE Catalogue
clothes, body, scrubbing, shoe, nail, washing-up, vegetable

Traidcraft
nail brush

Can Crushers

FoE Catalogue
The Green Shop Catalogue
Centre for Alternative Technology Catalogue
The Whole Thing Catalogue

Candles and Accessories

The Green Shop Catalogue
holders, extinguishers, tape-holder, night lights

Cleaning Products

FoE Catalogue
brass, silver, bathroom cleaners

The Green Shop Catalogue
washing-up liquid, fabric conditioner, toilet cleaner, car shampoo stain remover, oven-hood cleaner, dish-washer rinse-aid

Acdo Service Bureau
washing machine soap products

Centre for Alternative Technology Catalogue
septic tank conditioner

Design for a Healthy Environment
washing powder, washing up liquid, multi-surface cleanser
toilet cleanser, general purpose polish

Cloth Bags

FoE Catalogue
FoE Scotland - direct
The Green Shop Catalogue

Cloth Bags (cont'd)	Greenpeace Catalogue
	Traidcraft Catalogue unbleached calico and plastic bag storer
Clothes Airers	FoE Catalogue Domestic Paraphernalia Company
Clothing and Accessories	FoE Catalogue Greenpeace Catalogue Traidcraft Catalogue Women Working World-wide campaign for 'fair' clothes Traidcraft
Coffee	FoE Catalogue Greenpeace Catalogue *Wholefood Shops*
Cost Plugs and Savaplugs	FoE Catalogue The Green shop Catalogue
Cushions	Traidcraft FoE Catalogue One World Shop
Desk Lamp	FoE Catalogue Green Shop Catalogue
Doors	Victorian Pine original doors, shutters, room dividers
Duvets	FoE Catalogue Design For A healthy Environment
Energy Advice Centres	see addresses
Fire Lighters	FoE Catalogue
Flooring	Forbo-Nairn Ltd Wincanders Ltd Crucial Trading Fired Earth
Food and Drink	The Green Shop Catalogue coffee, tea, tea-bags, cocoa, raw cane sugar, Christmas cake
	The Whole Thing Catalogue sprouting beans
	Centre for Alternative Technology Catalogue organic wine
	Suma Wholefoods

Food and Drink (cont'd)

Traidcraft
Fair Trade catering Box, Christmas Hampers, dried product, cereal products, beverages, conserves

Green City Wholefoods
One World Shop
Organic Farms – see address list

Freeplay Radio

FoE Catalogue
needs no batteries

Furniture

Adventure Stuff
rocking chairs, coffee tables etc.

Design for a Healthy Environment
solid pine and beech furniture (farmhouse tables, chairs)

Revivals
furniture renovation

The Forest Workshop

Guttering

Marley Extrusions
Glynwed Foundries
Klober Ltd
Naylor Clayware
rainwater systems

Hot Water Bottle Alternative

FoE Catalogue

Kitchen Rolls

FoE Catalogue
Traidcraft Catalogue

Insulation

Green Home Catalogue
Warmcell Insulation (Approved Installers)
Out of Nowhere
Shetland Heatwise Ltd
Woodstone Developments
Everwarm Services
Centre For Alternative Technology Catalogue

Log Makers

FoE Catalogue
The Green Shop Catalogue
Centre for Alternative Technology Catalogue

Lighting and Lightbulbs

FoE Catalogue
The Green Shop Catalogue
Centre for Alternative Technology Catalogue

Matresses

see Beds

Mats

Traidcraft
natural jute mats

Nappies

FoE Catalogue

Nappies (cont'd) The Green Shop Catalogue
The Whole Green Thing

Nailbrushes FoE Catalogue

Organic Food FoE Catalogue
Green City Wholefoods
Traidcraft Catalogue
Organic Farms – see address list
Wholefood and Healthfood Shops

Paints Auro
natural organic paints

Osmo

Biofa
natural paints

Ecohaven
environmental paints

The Green Shop Catalogue
natural organic paints, primers, thinners, paint strip paste, paint and craft material for artists and children

The Nature Maid Company
natural paints and wood finish products

Design for a Healthy Environment
nutshell natural paints

Centre For Alternative Technology Catalogue

Paper-Towels The Green Shop Catalogue
Traidcraft Catalogue

Pest Control Centre for Alternative Technology Catalogue
humane mousetrap, flyball

Design for a Healthy Environment
household dust mite and allergen control sprays

Pillows Design For A Healthy Environment
FoE Catalogue

Polishes The Whole Thing
shoe, furniture

The Green Shop Catalogue
shoe, furniture, general purpose spray

Pottery Traidcraft
co-ordinated handthrown glazed earthenware (made in Zimbabwe)

Radiator Insulation Panels Centre For Alternative Technology Catalogue
DIY shops

Recycling Aladdink
recycles ribbon cassettes for computer printers

Recycling (cont'd)

Alcan
Aluminium Can Recycling Association

ICER

LEEP

Local Authorities – see address list

RNIB
aluminium foil recycling

Tayside Scrap Store

Rugs and Wall-Hangings

Jacquie Richardson
traditional rag rugs, wall-hangings, small pictures traditional hooking and clipping techniques

Traidcraft
screenprinted fringed cotton rugs

Sanitary Products

See Toiletries

Savaplugs

FoE Catalogue
The Green Shop Catalogue
Savawatt (UK) Ltd
DIY Shops

Shaving Products

FoE Catalogue
The Green Shop Catalogue
The Whole Thing Catalogue
The Body Shop

Solar Powered Lighting

The Centre For Alternative Technology
The Green Shop Catalogue

Stationery

FoE Catalogue
pens, refills, computer disks, stationary, diaries, re-usable labels, mouse mat, calendars,

Greenpeace Catalogue

The Green Shop Catalogue
writing pads, A4-refills, envelopes, memo-box, address books

Adventure Stuff
re-cycled stationary (made from out of date Ordinance Survey maps)

Traidcraft
handmade and childrens stationery, cards, gift wraps

Tablecloths

Greenpeace Catalogue
FoE Catalogue
Traidcraft

Tea

Traidcraft

FoE Catalogue
Greenpeace Catalogue

Tea (cont'd)
Greencity Wholefoods
Wholefood Shops

Toiletries
FoE Catalogue
shampoo, conditioners, seaweed bath, bath-salts, shaving products, sanity towels, tampons, soaps, toilet rolls, deodorant stone (roll-on, crystal)

The Green Shop Catalogue
soaps, liquid soap, shampoo, conditioners, seaweed foam bath and gel, toothpaste, deodorant-stone (roll-on), tampons, sanitary towels, panty shields, shower-cream, talc, toilet rolls

The Whole Thing
liquid natural soap, shampoo, conditioner, shaving cream, after shave lotion, sanitary products

Design for a Healthy Environment
protective hand cream

Toilet Cleaner
FoE Catalogue
The Green Shop Catalogue
Design for a Healthy Environment
Healthfood and Wholefood Shops

Toilet Paper
Traidcraft Catalogue
One World Shop
Healthfood and Wholefood Shops

Toothbrushes with Replaceable Heads
FoE Catalogue
The Green Shop Catalogue
Centre for Alternative Technology Catalogue

Toothpaste
FoE Catalogue
The Green Shop Catalogue
Healthfood and Wholefood Shops
The Body Shop

Towels
FoE Catalogue
cotton linen, organic cotton, children's hooded towel

Design for a Healthy Environment
Traidcraft
unbleached cotton

Trays
Traidcraft
wooden bed tray

Vacuum Cleaners
BEAM
Design for a Healthy Environment

Varnish and Wood Finish Products
Osmo

The Green Shop Catalogue
waxes, stains, preservatives, varnishes, shellac, yacht varnishes

Varnish and Wood Finish Products (cont'd)	Design for a Healthy Environment colour wood finishes, brush cleaner and thinner, wood fillers
Wallpaper Paste	Design For A Healthy Environment contains no fungicides or solvents
Washing-Up Liquid	FoE Catalogue Design For A Healthy Environment The Green Shop Catalogue *Wholefood and Healthfood Shops*
Washing-Up Brushes	FoE Catalogue
Water Saving	The Green Shop Catalogue
Wind Generators	The Green Shop Catalogue Centre For Alternative Technology Catalogue wind turbines, wind power accessories
Windows	S & P Windows Swedish Window Company Woodland Windows

Address List

Catalogues

The following organisations specialise in buying green by mail order and offer comprehensive catalogues.

Friends of The Earth
The Natural Collection Catalogue
Order Hotline 01225 442288

Centre for Alternative Technology
Unit 2
Bow triangle Business Centre
Eleanor street
London EH3 4NP
tel 0181 980 5580 fax 0181 980 2399

Green Shop Catalogue
Mail Order Department
The Green Shop
Bisley
Stroud
Gloucester GL6 7BX
tel 01452 770629 fax 01452 770629

Greenpeace
Canonbury Villas
London N1 2PN
tel 0171 354 5100 fax 0171 696 0012

The Healthy House
Coldharbour
Ruscombe
Stroud
Gloucester GL6 6DA
tel 01453 752216 fax 01453 753533

Traidcraft plc
Kingsway
Gateshead
Tyne & Wear NE11 0NE
tel 0191 491 0591

The Whole Thing
34 Market Place
Kendal LAP 4TN
tel 01539 721922 fax 01539 741199

ACDO
Imperial Works
Mallish Street
Ashley
Bolton BL1 8PP
tel 01204 309992

Main Addresses

Adventure Stuff
South Gate House
Dalmonach Works
Bonhill
Near Loch Lomond G83 9HN
tel/ fax 01389 711 010

Airsprung Scotland Ltd
Stepps Road
Queenslie Industrial Estate
Glasgow G33 4BY
tel 0141 774 3442

Alphabeds
of Dolbantau Mill
92 Tottenham Court Road
London WP1 9HE
tel 0171 636 6840 fax 0155 9395 496
tel 0155 9395 428 (Outside London)

Association of Environmentally Conscious Builders
F.A.O Sally Hall/Peter Warm
Nant-y-Garreg
Saron
Llandysul SA44 5EJ
tel 01559 370908

Aladdink
43 High Street
Eymouth
Berwickshire TD14 5EY
tel 018907 50965

Aluminium Can Recycling Association
176 Holiday Street
Birmingham B11 TJ
tel 0121 633 4656 fax 0121 633 4698

Auro Organic Paints
Unit 1
Goldstones Farm
Ashdown
Saffron Walden CB 2LZ

Biofa Natural Paints
5 School Road
Kidlington
Oxford OX5 2HB

Beam Built-In Vacuum Systems Ltd
St. Martins House
St. Martins Gate
Worcester WRI 2DU
tel 01905 611041/2 fax 01905 27462

Crucial Trading Ltd
Sales Office
The Market Hall
Craven Arms
Shropshire SY7 9NY
tel 01588 673666 fax 01588 673623

Centre for Alternative Technology
Unit 2
Bow triangle Business Centre
Eleanor street
London EH3 4NP
tel 0181 980 5580 fax 0181 980 2399

Cork Industry Federation
Beach House
57 Beach Road
Littlehampton
West Sussex BN17 5JH
tel 01903 721 6289

Domestic Paraphernalia Company
Unit 15 Marine Business Centre
Dock Road
Lytham FY8 5AJ
tel 01253 736334 fax 01253 795191

Energy Advice Centres

Tayside Advice Centre
7 Princes Street
Dundee DD4 6BY
tel 01382 453653

LEEP
72 Newhaven Road
Edinburgh EH5 6QG
tel 0131 555 4010 fax 0131 555 2768

Central Energy Advice Centre
72 Charlotte Street
Glasgow G1 5DW
tel 0141 552 0799

Orkney Energy Advice Centre
26 Junction Road
Kirkwall
Orkney KW15 1AG

Shetland Energy Advice Centre
Foula Start Centre
The Old School
Foula
Shetland ZE2 9PN
tel 01595 695468

Energy Advice Centres (cont'd)

Western Isles Energy Advice Centre
17 Francis Street
Stornoway
Isle of Lewis PA87 2NB
tel 01851 704300

Ecohaven
PO Box 149
Telford
Shropshire TF1 1YF

Environmental Paints
Unit 11
Dunscar Industrial Estate
Blackburn Road
Egerton
Bolton BL7 9PQ

Ecological Design Architects
F.A.O Heather Stopper
The British School
Flad Road
Stroud
Gloucestershire GL5 1QW
TEL 01453 765575

Fired Earth plc
Twyford Mill
Oxford Road
Adderbury
Oxon OX17 3HP
tel 01295 812088 fax 01295 810832

Forbo-Nairn Ltd
Linoleum Flooring
PO Box 1
Kirkcaldy
Fife SY7 9NA
tel 01592 261111

The Forest Workshop
Hillhouseridge
Shottkskirk Road'
Shotts
Lanarkshire ML7 4JS
tel 01501 822015 fax 01501 823919

Friends of The Earth Scotland
72 Newhaven Road
Edinburgh EH6 5QG
tel 0131 554 9977 fax 0131 554 8656

The FoE Natural Collection Catalogue
Order Hotline 01225 442288

Glynwed Foundries
Cast Iron Rainwater and Drainage
PO Box 3
Ketly
Telford
Shropshire TF1 4AD
tel 01952 641414 fax 01952 243760

Greencity Wholefoods
23 Fleming Street
Glasgow G31 1PQ
tel 0141 554 7633 fax 0141 556 5589

Green Shop Catalogue
Mail Order Department
The Green Shop
Bisley
Stroud
Gloucester GL6 7BX
tel 01452 770629 fax 01452 770629

Greenpeace
Canonbury Villas
London N1 2PN
tel 0171 354 5100 fax 0171 696 0012

The Healthy House
Coldharbour
Ruscombe
Stroud
Gloucester GL6 6DA
tel 01453 752216 fax 01453 753533

Hepworth Building Products
Clay Drainage
Hazelhead
Stocksbridge
Sheffield S30 5HG
tel 01226 763561 fax 01226 764827

ICER (Industry Council for Electronic Equipment Recycling)
6 Bath Place
Rivington Street
London EC2A 3JE
tel 0171 729 4766 fax 0171 729 9121

Jacquie Richardson
7 Ross Street
Golspie
Sutherland
tel 01408 633067

Klober Ltd
Copper Rainwater Goods
Peartree Ind. Estate
Upper Langford
Avon BS18 7DJ
tel 01934 853224 fax 01943 852221

Local Authorities

Aberdeen City Council
Town House
Broad Street
Aberdeen AB10 1FY
tel 01224 522000

Local Authorities (cont'd)

Aberdeenshire Council
Woodhill House
Westburn Road
Aberdeen AB16 5GB
tel 01224 682222

Angus Council
Council Headquarters
The Cross
Forfar DD8 1BX
tel 01307 461460

Argyll and Bute Council
Headquarters
Kilmory
Lochgilphead PA31 8RT
tel 01546 602127

Clackmannanshire Council
Greenfield
Alloa FK10 2AD
tel 01259 450000

Dumfries and Galloway Council
Council Offices
English Street
Dumfries DG1 2DD
tel 01387 261234

Dundee City Council
21 City Square
Dundee DD1 3BY
tel 01382 434000

East Ayrshire Council
Council Headquarters
London Road
Kilmarnock KA3 7BU
tel 01563 576000

Local Authorities (cont'd)

East Dumbartonshire Council
Tom Johnston House
Civic Way
Kirkintilloch
Glasgow G66 4TJ
tel 0141 776 9000

East Lothian Council
Council Buildings
Haddington EH14 3HA
tel 01620 827827

East Renfrewshire Council
Council Offices
Eastwood Park
Rouken Glen Road
Glasgow G46 6UG
tel 0141 621 3421

City of Edinburgh Council
City Chambers
High Street
Edinburgh EH1 1YG
tel 0131 529 7477

Falkirk Council
Municipal Buildings
Falkirk FK1 5RS
tel 01324 506070

Fife Council
Fife House
North Street
Glenrothes KY7 5LT
tel 01592 414141

Glasgow City Council
City Chambers
George Square
Glasgow G2 1DU
tel 0141 287 2000

Local Authorities (cont'd)

Highland Council
Glenurquhart Road
Inverness IV3 5NX
tel 01463 702000

Inverclyde Council
Municipal Buildings
Greenock PA15 1LY
tel 01475 724400

Midlothian Council
Midlothian House
Buccleauch Street
Dalkieth EH22 1DJ
tel 0131 663 2881

Moray Council
Council Offices
High Street
Elgin IV30 1BX
tel 01343 543451

North Ayrshire Council
Headquarters
Cunninghame House
Irvine KA12 8EE
tel 01294 324100

North Lanarkshire Council
PO Box 14
Civic Centre
Motherwell ML1 1TW
tel 01698 302222

Orkney Islands Council
Council Offices
Kirkwall KW15 1NY
tel 01856 873535

Local Authorities (cont'd)

Perth and Kinross Council
PO Box 77
1 High Street
Perth PH1 5PH
tel 01738 475000

Renfrewshire Council
Council Headquarters
Cotton Street
Paisley PA1 1LE
tel 0141 842 5000

Scottish Borders Council
Council Headquarters
Newton St. Boswells
Melrose TD6 0SA
tel 01835 824000

Shetland Islands Council
Town Hall
Lerwick ZE1 0HB
tel 01595 693535

South Ayrshire Council
County Buildings
Wellington Square
Ayr KA7 1DR
tel 01296 612000

South Lanarkshire Council
Council Offices
Almada Street
Hamilton ML3 0AA
tel 01698 454444

Stirling Council
Viewforth
Stirling FK8 2ET
tel 01786 443322

Local Authorities (cont'd)

West Dumbartonshire Council
Council Offices
Garshake Road
Dumbarton G82 3PU
tel 01389 737000

West Lothian Council
West Lothian House
Almondvale
Livingston EH54 6QG
tel 01506 777000

Western Isles Council/Comhairle Nan Eilean
Council Offices
Sandwick road
Stornoway
Isle of Lewis HS1 2BW
tel 01851 706022

Mailing Preference Service
Freepost 22
London W1W 7EZ

Marley Extrusions
Maidstone
Kent ME17 2DE
tel 01622 858888 fax 01622 858725

Montagne Jeunesse
London Production Centre
Broomhill Road
London SW18 4JQ

Northern Feather Home Furnishings Ltd
PO Box 1
Lockett Road
Ashton in Makerfield
Wiggan WN4 8DJ
tel 01942 721771 fax 01942 271321

Nature Maid Company
Unit D7
Maws Craft Centre
Jackfield
Ironbridge
Shropshire TF8 7LS
tel 01952 883288 fax 01952 883200

Naylor Clayware
Clay Drainage
Clough Green
Cawthorne
Barnsley S75 4AD
tel 01226 790591

One World Shop
St John's Church
Princes Street
Edinburgh EH2 4BJ
tel 0131 229 4541 fax 0131 221 0284

OSMO
Ostermann & Scheiwe UK Ltd
Osmo House
26 Swakeleys Drive
Ickenham
Middx UB10 8QD
tel 01895 234899 fax 01895 252171

Organic Farm Outlets

Harvest Moon Organic Produce
West Edingarioch Farm
Premnay
Insch AB52 6LP
tel 01464 20388
delivery service -weekly deliveries to Aberdeen, Edinburgh, Glasgow
fruit, vegetables, dairy products, cereal products

Organic Farm Outlets (cont'd)

Aberdeenshire Organic Producers
Blakehouse
Crudie
Turriff AB5 7FS
tel 01885 276
wholesale - normal office hours
fruit, vegetables

Mosspark
Lonmay
Fraserburgh AB4 4XH
tel 01346 532837
box scheme - opening times: phone for details
meat, poultry

Mr C J Ward
Bridgefoot
Mewmachar AB2 0PE
tel 01346 32837
delivery service - Fridays: Aberdeen area
vegetables

Paul van Midden
Murtle Farm & Garden
Crannoch Ree
Kingcausie Estate
Maryculter AB1 0AR
tel 01224 733778
farm gate - opening times: orders taken by phone -
for collection Tuesdays/Wednesdays
fruit, vegetables

A Hayman
Highland Harvest
3 Cairnleith Croft
Ythanbank
Ellon AB41 0UB
tel 01358 761298
farm gate/home delivery - opening times: generally once a week, phone for details
vegetables, potted herbs, pumpkins

Organic Farm Outlets (cont'd)

C M Leith & Son
Meikle Farm
Tillyeve
Udny
Ellon AB41 0SJ
tel 01651 842223
market stall - oats, potatoes, turnips

C J Ward
Bridgefoot
Newmachar AB2 0PE
tel 01651 862041
box scheme/home delivery - opening times: deliveries Friday - Aberdeen area
vegetables

L & M Allison
Sawmill Croft
Forglen
Turriff AB5 7JY
tel 01888 568501
farm gate - opening times: phone for details of availability/delivery
swedes (by the half tonne), vegetables, oats, Aberdeen Angus beef

Thistle Meat Company Ltd
Food Park
Burghmuir Drive
Blackhall
Industrial Estate
Invererurie AB51 9FS
tel 01467 22554
wholesale - opening times: normal office hours
meat

Parkgate Organic Nursery
Murryfield Cottage
Cumleys
Parkgate
Dumfries DG1 3NG
tel 01387 86391
farm gate - opening times: phone for details
fruit, vegetables, herbs, plants, garden supplies

Organic Farm Outlets (cont'd)

Sunrise Wholefoods
Station Yard
Kirkcuds DG7 1LA
tel 01556 504455
retail outlet/delivery service
cereal products, dried products, fruit, vegetables, prepared foods

Henderson's Farm Shop
92 Hanover Street
Edinburgh EH2 1DR
tel 0131 225 6694
retail outlet - opening times: Monday-Saturday 8.00 am - 7.00 pm
cereal products, dried products, fruit, vegetables, beverages, eggs, breads, pastries, alcohol

Natural Food Larder
205 Buntsfield Place
Edinburgh EH10 4DH
tel 0131 447 3033
retail outlet - opening times: Monday-Saturday 9.30 am - 5.30 pm
cereal products, fruit, vegetables, breads, pastries

Damhead Organically Grown Foods
32a Damhead
Old Pentland Road
Lothianburn
Edinburgh EH10 1EA
tel 0131 445 5591
farm shop/delivery service - opening times: Monday-Saturday 9.00 am - 5.00 pm
fruit, vegetables, meat, dairy, wholefoods

Natures Gate
83 Clerk Street
Edinburgh EH8 9JG
tel 0131 668 2067
Retail Outlet - opening times: Monday-Thursday 9.00 am - 7.30 pm
Friday-Saturday 9.00 am - 9.00 pm
cereal products, dried products, fruit, vegetables, beverages, prepared foods, dairy, conserves, bread, pastries, alcohol, non-food products

Organic Farm Outlets (cont'd)

Organic Farm Foods (Scotland) Ltd
Block 9
Whiteside Industrial Estate
Bathgate EH48 2DX
tel 01506 632911
wholesale - opening times: normal office hours
fruit, vegetables

New Leaf Health Food Shop
Argyle Place
Marchmont
Edinburgh EH9
tel 0131 228 8840

Real Foods Ltd
8 Brougham Street
Tollcross
Edinburgh EH3 9JS
tel 0131 228 1651
retail outlet - opening times: normal shop hours
wholefoods, cereals, pulses, dried products, dairy foods

Real Foods Ltd
37 Broughton Street
Edinburgh EH1 3JU
tel 0131 557 1911
retail outlet/mail order - opening times: normal shop hours
wholefoods, cereals, pulses, dried products, dairy products

Stirling Health Food Stores
22 Viewfield Street
Stirling FK8 10A
tel 01786 472490
retail outlet - opening times: Monday-friday 9.30 am - 5.00 pm
cereal products, dried products, fruit, vegetables

Stirling Health Food Stores
29 Dumbarton Road
Stirling FK8 2LQ
tel 01786 464903
retail outlet - opening times: Monday-friday 9.30 am - 5.00 pm
cereal products, dried products, fruit, vegetables

Organic Farm Outlets (cont'd)

Epo Growers
Old Edinbarnet
Hardgate G81 5BQ
tel 01389 75337
delivery service/market - opening times: phone for details
fruit, vegetables, potatoes

Evergreen Wholefoods Ltd
136 Nithsdale Road
Pollokshields G41 5RB
tel 0141 422 1303
retail outlet - opening times: Monday-Saturday 9.00 am - 6.00 pm
cereal products, dried products, fruit, vegetables, beverages, breads, pastries

Mellin's Health Food Store
713 Great Western Road
Hillhead G12 8QX
retail outlet - opening times: six days a week
cereal products, dried products, beverages, prepared foods, conserves, breads, pastries

Nairn Health Foods
1 Bridge Street
Nairn IV12 4EJ
tel 01667 453997
retail outlet - opening times: Monday-Saturday 9.00 am - 5.30 pm
cereal products, dried products, fruit, vegetables, prepared foods, eggs, conserves, bread, pastries, non-food products

Ayshire Organic Growers
The Walled Garden
Cushats
Sundrum-by-Ayr KA18 2LR
tel 01290 570631
box scheme - opening times: phone for details
fruit, vegetables

Butterworth's Organic Nurseries
Garden Cottage
Auchinleck Estate
Cumnock KA18 2LR
tel 01290 551088
mail order/delivery service - opening times: by arrangement
fruit trees

Organic Farm Outlets (cont'd)

Sundrum Organics
Unit 7
High House Industrial Estate
Auchinleck KA18 2LL
tel 01290 52020
mail order/delivery service - opening times: Monday-Friday 10.00 am - 10.00 pm
cereal products, dried products, fruit, vegetables, beverages, prepared foods, eggs, conserves, bread, pastries, non-food products (discounts for orders for orders over £30.00, free catalogue)

Sundrum Organics
Burnfoot Lodge
Barskimming
Mauchline KA5 5TB
tel 01290 52020
retail outlet - opening hours: normal shop hours
cereal products, dried products, wholefoods, pulses

Craigencalt Farm
Kinghorn
Bruntisland KY3 9YG
tel 01592 890078
farm shop - opening times: 9.00 am - 5.00 pm daily and on request
vegetables, herbs

Pillars of Hercules Farm Shop
Pillars of Hercules
Falkland
Cupar KY7 7AD
tel 01337 857749
farm shop - opening times: Monday-Saturday 10.30 am - 6.30 pm
vegetables, herbs, wholefoods

Golspie Mill
Golspie
Sutherland KW10 6RA
tel 01408 633278
mail order service - opening times: phone for details
water powered mill producing - stoneground flours and meals including bergmeal, peasemeal, rye, wheat flours

Organic Farm Outlets (cont'd)

Highland Health Stores
7 & 16 St. John Street
Perth PH1 5SP
tel 01738 628102
retail outlet - opening times: Monday-Saturday 9.00 am - 5.30 pm
cereal products, dried products, beverages, prepared foods, dairy, conserves, breads, pastries, non-food products

Mr & Mrs R M MacLaren
Glenearn
By Bridge of Earn
Perth PH2 9HL
tel 01738 812585
farm gate - opening times: phone for details
lamb, beef

South West Fullerton Farm
South West Fullerton
Meigle PH12 8SN
farm gate - opening times: by arrangement
fruit, vegetables, meat

Bean Machine
Greatridgehall
Kelso TD5 7PD
tel 01573 460346
delivery service - Edinburgh, Midlothian, Eastlothian, Borders - 24 hour answer-phone
cereal products, dried products, fruit, vegetables, prepared foods, breads, pastries

Out Of Nowhere
Old Tearie Farm House
Darnaway by Forres
Moray IV36 0ST
tel 01309 641524

Pukka Cloth
Head Office
174 Tower Bridge Road
London SE1
tel 0171 234 0000 fax 0171 234 0110

Revivals And Furniture Alternatives
76 Big Vennel
Cromarty
Ross-shire IV11 8XE
tel/fax 01381 600556

RNIB
tel 0131 557 4671

Savawatt (UK) Ltd
Sava Buildings
Waterloo Road
Bidford-on-Avon
Warickshire B5O 4JH
tel 01789 490413 fax 01789 490413

S & P Windows
Geoff Squires
31 Perrivale Close
Assart's Farm
Nuthall
Nottingham NG16 1QG
tel 01602 770868 fax 01602 770353

Suma Wholefoods
Dean Clough
Halifax HX3 5AN
tel 014222 345513 fax 01422 349429

Swedish Window Company
Earls Cone Industrial Park
The Airfield
Earls Cone
Colchester
Essex CO6 2NS
tel 01787 223031

Traidcraft plc
Kingsway
Gateshead
Tyne & Wear NE11 0NE
tel 0191 491 0591

Shetland Heatwise Ltd
Stanley Hill Offices
North Road
Lerwick
Shetland
tel 01595 696508 fax 01595 696568

Tayside Scrap Store Project
Lawside Road
Dundee DD3 6BJ
tel 01382 206241

Victorian Pine
Original Door Specialists
298 Buckley Road
London SE4 2RA
tel 0181 691 7162

Warmcel
Everwarm Services
7 Napier Square
Houstoun Industrial Estate
Livingston EH54 5DG
tel 01506 430456

Warmcell
Excell Industries Ltd.
12 Rassau Industrial Estate
Ebbw Vale
Gwent NP3 5SD
tel 01495 350655 fax 01495 350146

Wide Open Communications
6 Erskine Road
London NW3 3AJ
tel 0171 722 8207 fax 0171 722 6891

Woodwork
Bathgate Education Centre
Marjoribank Street
Bathgate EH48
tel 01506 654487

Woodstone Developments
1 Arthurfield Green
Kingskettle
Fife
tel 01337 831642 fax 01337 831489

Women's Environmental Network
Aberdeen Studios
22 Highbury Studios
London NE5 2EA
tel 0171 704 6800 fax 0171 354 1464

Women Working Worldwide
Centre for Employment Research
Room 126
MMU Humanities Build
Rosamond Street West
Manchester M15 6LL
tel 0161 247 1760 fax 0161 247 6333

The Whole Thing
34 Market Place
Kendal LAP 4TN
tel 0539 721922 fax 0539 741199

Woodland windows
1 Service Street
Cheadle Heath
Stockport SK3 OH2

Index

Publications from Friends of the Earth Scotland

This handbook has been written and published by Friends of the Earth Scotland who also publish a range of material on many different aspects of the environmental debate. Here is a selection. A full publications catalogue is also available, as is a catalogue for schools.

Send orders to FoE Scotland Publications Department, 72 Newhaven Road, Edinburgh, EH6 5QG, or ring 0131 554 9977 for further information. Prices include postage and packing. Please use codes when ordering.

The Green Office Action Plan – This step by step guide to greening your office will benefit both the environment and your business. The GOAP allows you to customise pages, to blow up pages into posters for display and update the directory of product and service suppliers every year. It is designed to help save money and tackle waste, and draws on sound independent environment research.
July 1996 **G19X** £24.95, (£19.95 to FoE members)

What On Earth – This bright and attractive 12 page publication is the campaign magazine of Friends of the Earth Scotland. Includes features, campaign updates and suggestions about what you can do to protect the environment.
Quarterly **G2X** £1.00

Protecting Our Environment – The unique citizen's guide to environmental rights and action, fully revised and updated covering the full range of local environmental issues - from getting your rubbish taken away or checking your drinking water, to campaigning against air pollution or using the planning system. Essential publication for individuals, Councils, community campaign groups, schools, libraries and environmental organisations.
New edition available June 97 **G1X** £4.95

How To Be A Friend Of The Earth – An easy and accessible guide for those wanting environmental tips. Energy efficiency, water pollution and recycling are just some of the areas covered.
October 1991 **G9Y** £3.45

25 Years for the Planet for People – An illustrated booklet giving a brief insight into the past 25 years of FoE International campaigns.
November 1996 **GO30I** £1.00

Towards a Sustainable Scotland – A comprehensive look at sustainability in Scotland using the concept of 'environmental space' to set targets for the next 15 and 50 years. Includes detailed statistics and case studies. Essential reading for community activists, local authorities, planners, development agencies, politicians, industrialists and anyone interested in sustainable development in Scotland.
March 1996 **S6X** £18 (£15 to FoE members)

Take the Heat Off the Planet! - How You Can Really Help to Stop Climate Change – This practical guide provides a clear explanation of the climate change problem. Easy instructions for achieving significant savings in energy use at home and work are combined with information on the barriers to energy efficiency which currently exist.
July 1993 **GW4Y** £3.45

Cars Cost The Earth – While the car is celebrating it's 100th anniversary, this briefing puts the full cost of the car into perspective.
January 1996 **T10Y** £0.50

Gardening Without Peat: The Friends of the Earth Guide to Peat Alternatives - In the last 30 years, commercial peat cutting for horticulture and gardening has become the greatest threat to the UK's remaining lowland bogs. This guide reviews the uses of peat and identifies alternatives.
March 1990 **C7Y** £6.95

Pack Back II: The Recyclables – Ever been annoyed because your shampoo bottle says it's recyclable but there is no where to recycle it? Following the success of the original Pack Back campaign on excess packaging, this campaign pack gives you a set of labels to return misleadingly-labeled packaging so that the manufacturers can recycle it. Also included are ideas for issues to include in letters to the manufacturers and retailers and our full briefing on 'Waste and Recycling'.
December 1996 **R12X** £1.50

Gender-Benders in the Bathroom – This campaign leaflet gives details of which toiletry products to avoid and which to buy if you are concerned about 'Gender-Bending' or hormone disrupting compounds.
November 1996 **R14X** £0.50

Consumers' Guide to Recycled Paper – A very useful, practical briefing which outlines the environmental arguments for using recycled paper. Explains how you can go about choosing a paper. Answers questions such as: What about paper for photocopiers and laser printers? Where can I buy it? What do eco-labels mean?
April 1993 **R1X** £0.50

Good Wood Guide – Fully updated version of our popular book looking at the types of wood available, where they come from, what environmental problems are associated with them and alternatives. Useful to builders, architects or DIY enthusiasts and designed to provide easy reference as well as containing more detailed background information.
December 1996 **TRF18Y** £5.95

Friends of the Earth Scotland Membership Information

Friends of the Earth Scotland is almost entirely funded by concerned individuals. To continue our work to protect the environment we need people like you to support us now. Please help us to meet the challenge of the 1990s by completing this form.

Name ______________________________

Address ______________________________

______________________________ Postcode ______________

YES, I'D LIKE TO JOIN FoE SCOTLAND.

Annual Membership

£19.50 ☐ **Family** **£14.50** ☐ **Waged**

£25 ☐ **Organisation** **£7** ☐ **Unwaged/Youth**

Paying by standing order

Your membership in the form of a monthly standing order will enable us to plan our campaigns even more effectively.

Yes I'll give a monthly sum of:

£10 ☐ **£5** ☐ **£3** ☐ **Other** ☐

Name of Bank/Building Society ______________________________

Address of Bank/Building Society ______________________________

______________________________ Postcode ______________

Account No. ______________________ Sort Code ______________

Signature ______________________ Start Date ______________

Bank Instructions: Please pay the above amount on the 18th of each month to Friends of the Earth Scotland, Account No. 00219943, Bank of Scotland, 2 North Junction Street, Edinburgh, EH6 6HN. Sort Code 80 02 32.
Quoting membership ref No: (For office use)

And / or I would like to make a Donation

£50 ☐ **£25** ☐ **£15** ☐ **Other** ☐

I enclose total £_____ cheque / postal order payable to Friends of the Earth Scotland or debit my Visa ☐ Access ☐ ☐

Card No. ☐☐☐☐ ☐☐☐☐ ☐☐☐☐ ☐☐☐☐

Expires: ☐☐ ☐☐ **Signature:** ______________

Please return this form to:

Friends of the Earth Scotland, 72 Newhaven Road, Edinburgh, EH6 5QG.
FoE Scotland Ltd. is a charity (no. SC03442)